Open Minds

Academic Freedom And Freedom Of Speech In Australia

Carolyn Evans And Adrienne Stone With Jade Roberts

16pt

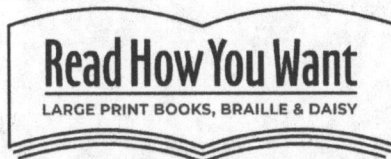

Read How You Want

LARGE PRINT BOOKS, BRAILLE & DAISY

Copyright Page from the Original Book

Published by La Trobe University Press in conjunction with Black Inc.
Level 1, 221 Drummond Street
Carlton VIC 3053, Australia
enquiries@blackincbooks.com
www.blackincbooks.com
www.latrobeuniversitypress.com.au

La Trobe University plays an integral role in Australia's public intellectual life, and is recognised globally for its research excellence and commitment to ideas and debate. La Trobe University Press publishes books of high intellectual quality, aimed at general readers. Titles range across the humanities and sciences, and are written by distinguished and innovative scholars. La Trobe University Press books are produced in conjunction with Black Inc., an independent Australian publishing house. The members of the LTUP Editorial Board are Vice-Chancellor's Fellows Emeritus Professor Robert Manne and Dr Elizabeth Finkel, and Morry Schwartz and Chris Feik of Black Inc.

NATIONAL LIBRARY OF AUSTRALIA

A catalogue record for this book is available from the National Library of Australia

Cover design by Akiko Chan
Text design and typesetting by Dennis Grauel
Author photos by Luke Marsden and Peter Casamento

Printed in Australia by McPherson's Printing Group.

TABLE OF CONTENTS

FOREWORD   i

ACKNOWLEDGEMENTS   x

INTRODUCTION   xiv

1: HISTORICAL CONFLICTS: STUDENT RADICALS AND PINK PROFESSORS   1

2: LAWS AND REGULATIONS PROTECTING ACADEMIC FREEDOM AND FREEDOM OF SPEECH   61

3: ACADEMIC FREEDOM   108

4: FREEDOM OF SPEECH AND ITS LIMITS   162

5: EMERGING THREATS: FUNDING MODELS AND RESEARCH PARTNERSHIPS   195

6: FOSTERING OPEN MINDS: SOME PRACTICAL OPTIONS   238

APPENDIX A: A SUMMARY OF THE 'REPORT OF THE INDEPENDENT REVIEW OF FREEDOM OF SPEECH IN AUSTRALIAN HIGHER EDUCATION PROVIDERS'   259

APPENDIX B: A CRITICAL REVIEW OF THE INSTITUTE FOR PUBLIC AFFAIRS' 'FREE SPEECH ON CAMPUS AUDIT 2018'   269

NOTES   275

BACK COVER MATERIAL   368

Index   371

FOREWORD

Glyn Davis

Some books are necessary, speaking to a moment when clarity is essential.

The issues of academic freedom and free speech on campus have been a target for clashes in the United States for some time. Recently, Australia imported the controversy, only lightly retooled for local consumption. Australian universities find themselves accused of suppressing the rights of staff and students, of creating a 'chilling' atmosphere that prevents the full flow of debate – indeed, of debasing the very idea of a university.

Cue columns about Cardinal John Henry Newman and knowledge for its own sake, demands for adopting a policy statement developed for the University of Chicago and claims of 'substantial hostility to free speech' on campus.

The chief, though by no means sole, proponent of this apparent crisis is the Institute of Public Affairs, its frequent pronouncements enthusiastically reprinted by *The Australian.* Pressed to act, in late 2017 education minister Dan Tehan announced the Independent Review of Freedom of Speech in Australian Higher Education Providers, to be led by former High Court chief justice and University of Western Australia chancellor Robert French.

There is irony in government deciding to investigate academic freedom. As *Open Minds* notes, government frequently emerges as the largest threat to such freedom. In controversies over nearly a century, politicians, police and security agencies, often in partnership with timid university administrations, are those most likely to subvert institutional autonomy and individual voices.

Nonetheless, French accepted the brief from Minister Tehan, and over several months consulted with university organisations, academics, students and the accreditation agency, first on the issues and then on a potential model code.

Like the assignment, the report findings proved somewhat contradictory.

On the one hand, French found clearly and unambiguously that IPA claims of a crisis had no substantive basis. 'Reported incidents,' he wrote, 'do not establish a systemic pattern of action by higher education providers or student representative bodies, adverse to freedom of speech of intellectual inquiry in the higher education sector.'

Yet despite finding no case to answer, French nonetheless recommended statutory amendments, including a legislated definition of academic freedom, amended higher education standards and a model code. Such changes, he argued, would strengthen protection of academic freedom and freedom of speech.

Minister Tehan accepted the recommendations from Justice French and called on universities to act. 'While recognising that universities are autonomous institutions,' he began, 'I am writing to all higher education providers to urge them to carefully consider Mr French's recommendations and the adoption of the Model Code.'

He would become more insistent in later media statements, criticising universities for using their autonomy. Universities, he claimed, are 'failing Australia' by choosing not to implement a 'voluntary' model code.

So although the independent review he commissioned found no evidence of systematic threats to academic freedom or freedom of speech on campus, and although the code was said to be a matter of institutional choice, here was the minister berating the sector for not accepting his preferred outcome.

And the Institute of Public Affairs? Though it produced no persuasive evidence of the claimed crisis in academic freedom for the inquiry, the attack on universities simply resumed.

Indeed the chair of the institute chose to ignore the key finding altogether. Responding to the French report, Janet Albrechtsen instead claimed vindication of her concerns, dismissed critics who suggested the institute was engaging in a culture war and once more censured universities for alleged failures despite a report that found just the opposite. Firmly held beliefs need brook no evidence.

Which brings us to *Open Minds,* a welcome alternative to endless assertions. Two of Australia's leading legal scholars tackle from first principles the issues of academic freedom and free speech on campus. Professors Carolyn Evans and Adrienne Stone bring scholarly rigour to the task. Their analysis is sympathetic to the approach pursued by French, if more wide-ranging in scope. Recent controversies are cited and examined, along with responses to the French report, but the underlying reasoning proceeds from the core concepts.

By opening the study with historic examples of institutional failure to protect academic freedom, the authors prove alive to risks and realities. There are threats to take seriously. Universities do not always live up to professed values.

The cases chosen sharpen the distinction Evans and Stone draw between academic freedom, defined by one vice-chancellor as a 'belief in free, critical and rational inquiry', and freedom of speech on campus. The first, necessarily, is restricted to academics:

an intrinsic part of the job rather than a separate right. There are, of course, arguments about limits and responsibilities, but *Open Minds* provides a precise delineation of academic freedom and its expression in institutional policies.

Freedom of speech, by contrast, is a general right open to students and staff alike. It is constrained by laws that apply across society, which must also operate on campus. Again, the concept is clearly outlined, along with controversies around hurtful speech and offensive speech. The authors acknowledge the gap that can arise between principle and expression in policy, particularly the challenge of writing disciplinary codes that seek to protect the collegial character of a university.

With the dual concepts of academic freedom and free speech firmly established, attention turns to threats. Once the risk was government intervention in academic appointments during the Cold War, or threats to public funding if management did not confront student protestors. The pressures now may be more subtle, but they are no less concerning. Treating students as customers can create worrying dynamics. Some foreign governments monitor activity on campus and complain loudly at any perceived insult, seeking therefore to influence curriculum. Caution is required when universities sign contracts with business for research funding or accept philanthropic grants with conditions that may undermine institutional autonomy.

Like most complex human interactions, freedoms are maintained by constant jostling and redefinition, contestation and defence. Yet there are practical ways universities can frame policies, beginning with principle and concluding with rules that give expression to ideals. Here, Evans and Stone step beyond analysis. Both are influential voices in the discussion of academic freedom and occupy positions from which they shape practice.

Carolyn Evans is a distinguished specialist in religious freedom and the law, a former dean of the Melbourne Law School and now vice-chancellor at Griffith University. She is responsible for ensuring that institution, alone and as a voice within the broader sector, lives those values expressed in formal policy statements.

As a Kathleen Fitzpatrick Australian Laureate Fellow and director of the Centre for Comparative Constitutional Studies, Adrienne Stone is a national voice for accuracy in expression and action around academic and speech freedoms. She was invited to edit the international handbook on freedom of speech for Oxford University Press, which is both recognition of expertise and an opportunity to influence thinking around the globe.

For a long time, academic freedom was an undocumented expectation of behaviour on campus. Along with institutional autonomy, it was accepted as a necessary licence so scholars could research and teach knowledge without constraint. Recent controversies demand what was once implicit now be codified, with all the risk for nuance and shading.

If principles must become words able to guide practice, then academic freedom and free speech on campus need explication by scholars deeply imbued in the concepts, alive to their multiple and overlapping meanings. Even better when principles are set in context and expressed with concision and style, complete with examples for those seeking policy guidance. In *Open Minds,* we find these ambitions admirably realised.

And so this is a necessary book, speaking to a difficult moment for universities, providing clarity and support for fundamental freedoms on campus.

Glyn Davis is CEO of the Paul Ramsay Foundation, and Distinguished Professor of Political Science at the Australian National University. He was the vice-chancellor of the University of Melbourne from 2005 to 2018.

ACKNOWLEDGEMENTS

This volume is the product of the long academic association and friendship of its principal authors. Its subject matter is especially close to our hearts. As scholars of constitutional law teaching at the University of Melbourne, our respective interests lay in freedom of religion and freedom of speech. The obvious overlap led us to many conversations about ideas of tolerance, offensiveness and freedom. At the same time, it was impossible to ignore how the concepts central to our scholarly lives were playing out in the university around us. In these issues we have a personal stake as well as an intellectual interest.

Our careers have diverged since we first explored these issues. Carolyn Evans' career took her from leadership positions at the University of Melbourne to Griffith University as its vice-chancellor, while Adrienne Stone continues as a scholar, teacher and research centre director at Melbourne Law School. However, with the generous support of the Australian Research Council's Discovery grant scheme, we have been able to collaborate on this project. We were most fortunate to have the support of Jade Roberts, a researcher at Melbourne Law School. Jade's meticulous research, keen analytical mind and impeccable organisation have made an enormous contribution to the book, and it would never have been completed without her. We also acknowledge the support of colleagues who have discussed and, in the spirit of the book, argued with us over many years. One of the pleasures of writing about universities is the interest it attracts from colleagues across the academy.

In 2019, Adrienne Stone delivered the Fay Gale Lectures for the Academy of Social Sciences in Australia to audiences in Melbourne and Adelaide. These lectures developed some of the ideas expressed in chapters 3 and 4 and were greatly improved by discussions with colleagues in attendance. She also benefited from an opportunity to discuss these issues on Glyn Davis's podcast, *The Policy Shop,* and at the Australian National University's Summit on Academic Freedom and Academic Autonomy in December 2018. She is grateful to many colleagues for the benefit of informal discussions, including Sean Cooney, Patrick Emerton, Simon Evans, Katharine Gelber, Tarunabh Khaitan, Ronan McDonald, Julian Sempill and Jayani Nadarajalingam. She would like to acknowledge her parents, Margaret and Jonathan Stone, whose commitments to free speech and academic inquiry have been a lifelong inspiration, and Graeme Hill for his encouragement and support.

Carolyn Evans is grateful to her vice-chancellor colleagues and the leadership team at Griffith University, with whom she has enjoyed robust discussion and debates about the practical implementation of freedom of speech and academic freedom in university policies. She was fortunate to present some of the ideas in this book at a workshop on academic freedom at Melbourne University, held jointly with King's College London and the University of Chicago. She is grateful to workshop participants for their feedback and insights. She is also grateful to her husband, Stephen Donaghue, and her children, for their patience with this project and their willingness to discuss its central ideas.

We are both profoundly grateful to Glyn Davis for his willingness to write the foreword to this volume.

A final word of thanks is due to La Trobe University Press and Black Inc. for the decision to publish this book and their assistance throughout the writing and editing process. We are grateful beneficiaries of the wisdom, energy, patience and vision of the editorial team.

INTRODUCTION

The past few years have seen controversies about academic freedom and freedom of speech at Australian universities erupt at regular intervals. Debate has centred on two incidents in particular.

The first was James Cook University's dismissal of geophysicist Peter Ridd in May 2018, which came after his public criticism of the research being carried out by the university's Centre of Excellence for Coral Reef Science and the Australian Institute of Marine Science. The dismissal of Ridd, who was well known for his climate-change scepticism, made headlines, and some commentators interpreted it as deliberate interference with Ridd's academic freedom. The university denied these accusations and said Ridd was fired because he repeatedly breached its code of conduct, both by the manner in which he publicly criticised his colleagues and by disclosing confidential details of directions the university imposed on him in the course of an internal investigation. Although the Federal Circuit Court ruled that the university had unfairly dismissed Ridd and breached the commitment to intellectual freedom laid out in its enterprise agreement, the full Federal Court upheld his termination on appeal, and further proceedings in the High Court may yet ensue.[1]

The second incident was the student protests that arose in response to Bettina Arndt's planned appearance at the University of Sydney in September 2018. Arndt, an author and sex therapist, had been invited to speak on campus by the university's Liberal Club as part of her 'Fake Rape Crisis Campus Tour', which contested the scale of the issue of sexual assault on university campuses.[2] Small protests had accompanied her appearance at La Trobe University in Melbourne earlier that month, and her arrival at the University of Sydney was met by about forty protesters, who attempted to block attendees from entering the venue.[3] The police were called, the protesters were dispelled and Arndt's speech went ahead. Speaking about the events on radio station 2GB two weeks later, Arndt condemned the protesters as an 'unruly mob of abusive students' and urged the university to hold the organisers accountable.[4] During an interview with broadcaster Alan Jones, she framed the protests as a freedom of speech issue: 'Today's conservatives aren't interested in shutting down free speech, they're trying to promote it. And the left, amazingly, is all in favour of silencing people expressing views they don't like.'[5]

The furore that greeted these two incidents gained momentum, inspiring claims from those on the right of the political spectrum that Australian universities were increasingly censorious, prone to limiting the diversity of ideas on campus and generally highly intolerant, especially towards conservative thought.[6] This political campaign was catalysed by the Institute of Public Affair's 'Free Speech on Campus Audit 2018' (examined in appendix B), which attempted to rank universities by their degree of support for freedom of speech. The audit's claims were reported by the conservative media and echoed by such think tanks as the Centre for Independent Studies.[7] Conservative politicians, such as Liberal senator James Paterson, used them to argue that funding should be stripped from universities.[8]

The campaign – particularly as it related to on-campus freedom of speech – was somewhat derivative. It was clearly influenced by comparable political campaigns in the United States and tended to rely heavily on reports of American controversies to supports its theories, in addition to the few relevant Australian incidents it could point to. But despite its lack of evidence, the campaign was influential.[9] At the end of 2018, education minister Dan Tehan announced that an independent review of the rules and regulations protecting intellectual inquiry and freedom of speech on university campuses was to be undertaken, headed by the Hon. Robert French, chancellor of the University of Western Australia and a former chief justice of the High Court.[10]

The Independent Review and its findings, which are explored in chapter 2, led to some modest regulatory change in Australia, but even as we finished this book during the coronavirus pandemic of 2020, universities were never far from the headlines and even the courts.[11] On the one hand, university researchers led the response to the pandemic. Immunologists and epidemiologist were no doubt the most prominent, but the crisis was of such depth that the response required broad disciplinary expertise. Across the sciences, social sciences and humanities, university researchers were at the forefront, helping all of us to understand and respond to the deep social, political, economic and moral challenges we faced.[12] On the other hand, old worries about freedom in universities continued.

Murdoch University settled proceedings against an academic member of the university senate who had criticised its admissions procedures, but a clear resolution of the questions of academic freedom at the heart of the dispute was not reached, and Peter

Ridd lost his case against James Cook University in the Full Court of the Federal Court.[13] As the world order shifted in response to the pandemic, concerns about foreign influence and free speech in Australian universities became ever more acute. The University of Queensland suspended a student leader and member of its university senate for misconduct, sparking claims (denied by the university) that it had suspended him for anti-China activism. Legal action is pending.[14]

The first aim of this book is to provide the basis for better public discussion by providing some context for these events and an accessible account of the regulatory environment in which universities actually operate. In this respect, it is especially important, we think, to focus on Australia. As scholars of freedom of religion and freedom of speech, we have long been acutely aware of the tendency of Australians to absorb, as if by osmosis, the tenor of American debates. As universities assumed centre stage in public discourse, we again saw this frustrating dynamic. While this book is informed by the debates and events in other countries, we hope that it serves a useful purpose in its clear focus on Australian history, law and culture as they are relevant to speech in our universities.

The book's opening chapter is designed to serve as a reminder that there has never been a golden age of openness, freedom and tolerance in Australian universities. These values have always faced challenges from government, university leadership, students and academics – all of whom, at different times, have also come to their defence. Claims that intolerant radical students these days have lost sight of the values that sustain university life are at least a century old. Indeed, the climate in universities is currently considerably quieter than during other periods. Equally, the pressure on academics who hold unconventional views or are in conflict with their university is familiar and was especially acute during the Cold War of the middle of the last century.

Though we do not want to dismiss the seriousness of problems now facing

Australian universities, this chapter serves as a plea for perspective. It reminds us that governments have the potential to be a serious threat to academic freedom, given their power to interfere in university matters. The greatest contemporary challenge to the Australian university may lie not in the antics of a small number of students but in the pressures brought to bear by external influence of various kinds to which universities are rendered vulnerable by a lack of funding.

In the book's second chapter, we turn to the Australian regulatory landscape, which is a complex mix of Commonwealth and state laws, administrative oversight and internal university policies and processes. The chapter sets out, as simply as possible, the basic requirements of the leading Commonwealth law (the *Higher Education Support Act 2003*), the operation of the Tertiary Education Quality and Standards Agency, university-specific legislation (usually state laws) and internal governing mechanisms, which include university policies and enterprise agreements. It also assesses the Independent Review and concludes by examining positions taken in the United Kingdom, the United States and Canada, as a way of illustrating alternative legal approaches to protecting academic freedom and freedom of speech in universities.

One of the issues we identify in chapter 2 is the uncertainty created by the term 'free intellectual inquiry' in the Commonwealth governing legislation and the term 'intellectual freedom' in some enterprise agreements. We recognise the potential of these terms to cause confusion, and we endorse the suggestion that 'free intellectual inquiry' be replaced with 'academic freedom and freedom of speech' in Commonwealth legislation.

This brings us to a larger point: academic freedom and freedom of speech are often treated as synonymous. The second aim of the book is to untangle these concepts and to explain the relationship between them. Academic freedom is the principle that protects the most important and distinctive function of the university – the advancement and dissemination of knowledge. But universities are also institutions of civil society, and in this capacity freedom of speech is valuable for its service to democratic government, personal freedom and dignity. Over the course of chapters 3 and 4, we set out this distinction and make our central argument that the unique role of universities justifies the primacy of academic freedom. While freedom of speech will always be important, in shaping its limits and articulating its boundaries, universities can and should consider academic values first.

In chapter 3, we develop an account of academic freedom that follows from the essential purpose of a university. As we argue, university research and teaching contribute greatly to public wellbeing, both directly, though the pursuit and dissemination of knowledge, and indirectly, through support for free democratic government. To perform this role, universities in turn require freedom in research and teaching, broadly conceived, and an appropriate level of independence from government and other external influences.

Having stated the principle in outline, we then consider what it means in practice by focusing on the issue of public commentary by academic researchers, a context in which the two freedoms are sometimes confused. As we show, there are two circumstances in which academics should be understood to be relying on academic freedom: when speaking within their broad area of expertise and when commenting on or criticising university governance. In contrast, when academics make general public comments that are not informed by their academic expertise, we argue that academics are exercising their right to freedom of speech.

The distinction is important, because although academic freedom is narrower than a general right to freedom of speech, it is also stronger. When relying upon academic freedom, the position of academics is (or at least should be) quite different from the position of others. Specifically, academics ought to have much more freedom than other employees of universities to discuss their work and ideas and to criticise university governance. When exercising ordinary free speech rights, however, academics are more or less in the same position as other citizens and, specifically, other employees of universities. This still leaves them with a considerable and broad scope of free speech, but it is subject to a wider variety of justifiable limitations.

In chapter 4, we consider the issue of freedom of speech in universities. We reiterate and elaborate on the importance of this freedom as a political value, yet we seek to show that the controversy over freedom of speech in universities occurs within quite a narrow domain. First, speech in universities must be *legal.* Academics, staff and students have no greater right than anyone else to defame, threaten, engage in racial and religious vilification, obstruct public roads or occupy public space in the name of freedom of speech. Second, it follows from our argument in chapter 3 that much expressive activity in universities – activity that is part of, or closely related to, teaching and research – falls within the ambit of academic freedom rather than freedom of speech. For the most part, free speech questions in universities arise within what we call the 'public square' of the university. That is, they arise in relation to expressive activity in public areas, at public events or in the course of other activities that are not part of the university's teaching and research mission – for example, student protests or public lectures by controversial speakers.

Typically, a spirit of openness and lively debate will promote just the kind of environment in which academic inquiry will also thrive. In most respects, therefore, the reasons to limit speech in universities resemble the principles that govern it elsewhere in the public realm. Speech should only be limited where it causes a sufficiently serious form of harm, and rules limiting freedom of speech should be impartially drawn, fairly enforced, no broader than necessary and reasonably clear. Moving into more controversial territory, we accept the prospect that speech that could cause serious emotional harm (not mere offence) may sometimes justify limiting freedom of speech, a position that is widely accepted internationally.

In addition, we think that there are circumstances – hopefully rare – where speech may interfere with the environment necessary for teaching and research. Where speakers flagrantly disregard or undermine academic values, where they advance obviously untrue and even dangerous ideas, or where they attack or denigrate a group within the university, the environment for research and teaching is damaged not promoted. In such cases, there is an especially strong case for universities to take action to defend academic values, though of course they must act with care and proportion.

The broad principles relating to freedom of speech are of course easier to state than apply, and the chapter also considers difficult practical questions like the costs incurred by controversial speakers in universities, the use and potential misuse of disciplinary codes, and the difficult line between robust debate and harassment and bullying. The final aim of this book is to address these and other difficult questions that universities face as they seek to uphold academic freedom and freedom of speech while recognising their limits.

In chapter 5, we address the challenging context of globalisation and commercialisation that has dramatically reshaped the way universities are funded. Students are paying more for their degrees; the student body is increasingly international; more and more research funding comes from philanthropic donations and commercial and governmental partnerships. Some of these trends have no doubt contributed to their rapid rise in international standing.[15] But they also place pressures on universities, as students, research partners and governments (including foreign governments) seek to influence research, teaching and public discussion in universities.

We argue that universities are right to capitalise on the opportunities that arise but must do so with a clear sense of the university's fundamental purpose. Universities need to educate their staff and students about academic freedom and free speech, and they need to work with commercial and governmental partners to ensure these values are well understood and respected in partnership arrangements.

In chapter 6, we conclude by considering how universities might promote these values and their understanding. The two most prominent models available to and pressed upon them are the much-discussed Chicago Principles and the Model Code produced by the Independent Review. We assess these models and argue that they are useful starting points but we would expect Australian universities to adopt the kinds of ideas presented to their own specific contexts.

The overriding tenor of the book is, we hope, optimistic. We are determined idealists. Universities are not simply forums for the politics of society at large. They are not commercial institutions, nor are they instruments of government. They are special communities dedicated to teaching and research. Their challenges are many and complex, but we believe it is essential, and also possible, for universities to be faithful to the core ideals of the university, even in the modern globalised and commercialised age.

1

HISTORICAL CONFLICTS: STUDENT RADICALS AND PINK PROFESSORS

On 4 May 1932, *The Age* reported that tensions between Labor Club members and other students at the University of Melbourne had boiled over into a series of incidents on campus. A large group of medical students were outraged by seditious comments allegedly made by a student and Labor Club member named Mr Ingwerson, including a statement that the British flag was 'saturated with the blood of martyrs'. An angry mob ambushed Mr Ingwerson while he ate lunch at a university cafeteria, but he escaped with the help of friends. Later that day, 'several hundred' students gathered outside the Labor clubhouse. Three of its members attempted to barricade themselves in the office of the student newspaper, *Farrago,* but were seized and 'rushed through a lane formed by the students from the clubhouse door to the lake, into which [they] were thrown'.[1]

The Age described the scene by the lake:

> While they were standing in about 18 inches of water, the crowd of over 1000 students sang the national anthem, and gave cheers for the King and the British Empire, and hoots for the Communist Party. They refused to allow the ... students to come out of the lake until they had also sung the national anthem.[2]

The article goes on to note that 'several policemen were present during the ducking, but did not interfere'. A spokesperson for the mob 'said that the demonstration was intended as a gesture to the Communistic element in the university to show that it would not be permitted to interfere with activities that were not in harmony with its own'.[3] In an announcement published in *Farrago,* Professor W.E. Agar, president of the professorial board, was equivocal in his condemnation of the dunking, suggesting some responsibility lay with the Labor Club students themselves.[4]

As this glimpse of an earlier era shows, universities have long been sites of conflict between students, staff, the political classes and the wider community. From medieval times, when universities were built like fortresses as protection against the townsfolk, who commonly clashed with students, to the current moment, when the pros and cons of deplatforming controversial on-campus speakers are widely debated, the history of universities is replete with examples of political tension, acrimonious debate and even violence. As a result, the scope of academic freedom and the nature of free speech in universities have long been contested issues.

We sometimes hear claims that free speech and academic freedom are in a particularly perilous state in these early decades of the twenty-first century.

Students are characterised as intolerant of different points of view, in contrast to previous generations, who enjoyed a vigorous intellectual debate, and academic freedom is said to be under unprecedented attack from the forces of political correctness. On the basis of three studies over a three-year period, the Institute for Public Affairs, a conservative public-policy think tank, claims that 'the majority of Australia's universities limit the diversity of ideas on campus' and 'there is evidence of increasing censorship at Australia's universities'.[5]

However, in considering such claims, we would do well to recall that freedom of speech and academic freedom in Australian universities have been controversial issues for at least a century and have at times been debated on a larger scale and with far greater intensity than they are today. We might also remember that threats to these freedoms have come from both the political left and the political right, and that Australia has tended to avoid the harsher repressiveness seen in other countries. It is sobering to learn about the ways in which illiberal governments around the world have attacked universities as part of orchestrated campaigns of wider political and social repression, and there are examples of liberal democracies with poor records too.[6]

The historical treatment of universities at home and elsewhere in the world has much to teach us about the importance of protecting academic freedom and free speech from opponents inside and outside the academy. This chapter gives an overview of several periods in Australia's history in which free speech and academic freedom were put under serious pressure. Trends can be seen. In the early and mid-twentieth century, when the student body was largely conservative, it was left-wing students and academics who came under attack from the government and sometimes other students and staff. It was then the Labor Party that defended intellectual freedom. Over the decades, this dynamic shifted and now students and faculty are more often associated with left-wing and progressive causes, while accusations of intolerance and censorship, and claims that intellectual freedom is under attack, typically come from conservative voices.

The intensity of the debate on these issues, in government and within universities, has also differed over time, as has the willingness of various university leaders to defend the rights of students and staff. Yet there are uncanny echoes in the public condemnation of students and faculty across the decades. Aspects of our language may have changed, but many of the tactics deployed to silence dissenting voices have a long lineage.

Prewar Debates

In the first half of the twentieth century, pacificism and the rise of communism and fascism were hotly debated issues in Australian universities. Pacifism had many proponents in the lead-up to World War I, but the Australian government and many others saw it as a serious threat to the country's military strength. Academics who vocally opposed war were strongly criticised by the government and the public.[7] As early as 1902, Professor George Wood, the co-founder of the Australian Anti-War League, was censured by the senate of the University of Sydney, following widespread criticism of his public comments against the Boer War.[8]

Australia's engagement in World War I brought these tensions to a head, with pacifists and anti-conscription campaigners, including individuals from within the academy, being treated with hostility by the government and many members of the public. As the war progressed and casualties mounted, Australia's participation became more unpopular with the general population, who voted down conscription in two plebiscites.[9] It was this context that gave rise to the case of Vere Gordon Childe, which has been described as 'one of the earliest instances of the intervention of the state in academic appointments in Australia'.[10]

Childe studied at Queen's College, Oxford, from 1915 to 1917, an experience that strengthened his existing socialist and pacifist views.[11] On his return to Australia, Childe campaigned against the introduction of conscription and as a result of his activism was subjected to surveillance by the Department of Defence and had his mail censored.[12] He secured a position as a senior resident tutor at the University of Sydney's St Andrew's College in November 1917, but he kept the role for little more than six months. At Easter in 1918, Childe addressed a peace conference and in May of the same year the college principal requested he resign, which he did.[13] Colleagues who sympathised with Childe's situation attempted to find other work for him at the university, but in July the university senate refused to appoint him as a tutor in ancient history, apparently on advice from the defence department that his appointment during wartime was undesirable.[14]

William McKell, a member of parliament in New South Wales and future leader of the Australian Labor Party, raised the issue in parliament, questioning the university senate's decision and the legality of Childe's treatment.[15] Such protests were to no avail, however, and in 1921, having worked as a schoolteacher and as a speechwriter and private secretary to Labor politician John Storey, Childe left Australia for England, where he went on to have a successful academic career in archaeology.[16]

The period between the two world wars was also a tumultuous one, and increasing global tension – resulting from the rise of both fascism and communism in 1930s Europe – led to heated discussions on Australian campuses. On 22 March 1937, the University of Melbourne hosted a debate on the Spanish Civil War, organised by the university's debating society, which examined the contention 'that the Spanish Government is the ruin of Spain'. The debate pitted the Catholic student group, the Campion Society, against the university Labor Club and Catholic Party.[17]

Australian historian Manning Clark was in the audience and paints a memorable picture of the scene:

Early in 1937 I had a refresher course in tribal loyalty ... To my surprise I entered a room occupied by two howling mobs – one for and one against the Spanish government. It was like being in the outer at a game between Carlton and Collingwood ... Before the chairman and the speakers entered the theatre the exchanges between [supporters of either side] were lost in the uproar. Some students ran over the roof to add to the hubbub and noise in the theatre. The chairman ... called for order ... But his appeals fell on deaf ears.[18]

Some parties expressed concern that on-campus free speech was under threat. Dubbing the debate a 'Spanish bull fight', *Farrago* reported that the debate's external speaker, the Reverend J. Gray Robertson, could hardly be heard over the 'vocal barrage put up by a section of the audience'.[19] In a letter to the editor published in the same issue, a reader complained of 'the ill-mannered interruption' of Robertson:

The truth or falsehood of the speaker's statements is quite beside the point; he has come at the invitation of three university societies, and deserved at least the courtesy of a hearing. To unite strong feelings with tolerance of opposed views is not easy, but if this happy union is denied in a university, where can we hope to find it?[20]

In the wake of the debate, Vice-Chancellor Raymond Priestly called for more tolerance and objectivity in the discussion of current events:

I am a keen supporter of free speech and free discussion in a university. Nevertheless, I have viewed with some dismay certain manifestations arising out of the discussion of social and political questions here, particularly recently. One is a certain intolerance which I believe to be incompatible with dispassionate and unbiased examination of the facts and reasoned discussion and which, it seems to me, have been shown by both sides.[21]

Priestly went on to urge students to conduct themselves more civilly in future and to focus on the intellectual value of whatever subject was up for debate:

> Debate thorny questions with good humour, sense of proportion, balance and reasonableness and without undue rancour and heat. Allow your intellect and not your passions to prevail. If you have visitors from outside treat them with courtesy and by your own example encourage them to behave.[22]

Despite his professed dismay at the debate's fallout, Priestley defended the university against sweeping criticism of its politics, insisting that it was far less extreme than Cambridge. He described Melbourne's left in the 1930s as a small and inactive faction, its radical reputation an invention of the conservative press's fertile imagination. 'I often think,' Priestley observed, 'that if Cambridge University was put down in Melbourne, this place would go up in flames.'[23]

The Anti-Communist Era

Following the defeat of fascism and Nazism in World War II, and the breakdown of the alliance between the Soviet Union and the Western Allies, the Menzies government became increasingly concerned about communism in Australia. Just as McCarthyism targeted American universities in its attempts to hound communists out of public life, Australia's universities were seen as especially vulnerable to communist infiltration, and over time they were subjected to increasing levels of government scrutiny and interference.[24] In addition to the official interventions that led to the repression of academic freedom, the 'climate of political repression and profound conservatism [that] dominated public debate' also had an impact.[25] That influence can be discerned in the controversy that erupted at the University of Melbourne in September 1951.

The episode began when students and staff attended a meeting to discuss the referendum on banning the

Australian Communist Party called by the Menzies government the previous month. Staff and students present at the meeting voted strongly against the proposed referendum. This led the University Council to voice concern that the views expressed at such meetings could be falsely construed as the views of the university. Suspecting that the university had plans to ban similar meetings in the future, students reacted angrily. The Council's comments were also publicly criticised in an editorial in *The Argus*.[26]

In response to the criticism, Chancellor Charles Lowe attempted to justify the University Council's views. He expressed his surprise at the historical permissiveness of the university's 'long-standing practice [of] allowing members of the staff to organise meetings on university premises without any assent from the vice-chancellor ... to discuss any question whatsoever'. Lowe argued that such a position could no longer be tolerated: 'The Council has responsibility for the university premises and such a practice is really an abdication of control.'[27]

Lowe's tenacious defence of the Council's stance led to a statement on the issue from the state's Labor premier, John Cain, who stressed that the government 'would not tolerate stifling of free speech'.[28] Lowe responded to this charge in the University of Melbourne's *Gazette,* arguing that when a university facilitates a discussion of public issues it has a duty to ensure all sides of an issue are represented and that students are not unduly influenced by the views of professors, who 'inside the university and to university students ... [cannot] rid [themselves] of the prestige and authority', which they derive from their positions. Lowe went on to stress that he had no intention of limiting the public statements of professors 'outside the university'.[29]

Government Interference

It is not always possible to trace the effect that anti-communist government policy and public sentiment had on academic life during the first half of the twentieth century. Scholars who espoused left-wing views were certainly denied academic positions by conservative or simply cautious university leaders, but the reasoning behind these decisions was rarely transparent.[30] We do know, however, that the Australian Security Intelligence Organisation (ASIO) systematically engaged with the leadership of universities to limit the influence of left-wing or subversive views on campus. And by the beginning of the 1950s, the suspicious atmosphere of the Cold War emboldened government intervention in university appointments.

According to historian David McKnight, ASIO could not directly 'veto or vet staff appointments' as it might have wished to, but wherever possible it 'hamper[ed] the work of academics who it regarded as "security threats" and, on occasions, actually stopped academic appointments'.[31] For the most part, university leaders went along with this willingly, if not always happily. Media historian Fay Anderson notes that 'university administrators monitored communists and liberals on campus long before ASIO began its intense and official campaign of surveillance of "suspect" intellectuals'.[32]

In March 1952, ASIO director-general Colonel Spry ordered an investigation of all academics employed at Australian universities.[33] 'I am sure that you will readily appreciate,' he wrote to Prime Minister Robert Menzies, 'the inadvisability of employing, in any university, lecturers who are likely to infect students with subversive doctrines.'[34] Menzies is subsequently thought to have authorised the investigation of all applicants for fellowships and other academic appointments at the Australian National University. Evidence exists of a letter written by Colonel Spry informing Menzies that ANU had 'unofficially' submitted the names of its applicants to ASIO for review.[35] When ANU vice-chancellor Douglas Copland was contacted about this arrangement, he told Menzies that the Council was unhappy that applicants were subjected to a political test but could ensure that 'in general, persons who are suspected of being a security risk will not be appointed to responsible positions'.[36]

ASIO's informants, many of whom were students or academics, reported on aspects of academics' conduct, including the public language they used, which was believed to betray any subversive tendencies.[37] Some informants were compensated for the information they provided, while others volunteered it, motivated, perhaps, 'by patriotism, strong anti-communist sentiment or simple malice'.[38]

The result of ASIO's investigation was the creation of a list of 'subversive intellectuals' on whom it would keep intelligence files. According to its records, even ASIO acknowledged that the lists may have been overinclusive.[39] At Melbourne University alone, sixty-three academics, or 9 per cent of its staff of seven hundred, were recorded in the file:

> The sixty-three academics were divided into categories with A denoting CPA membership, B those 'suspected on reasonably well-found grounds of membership', C was 'Communist Party sympathisers' and

D was 'all other persons recorded by ASIO about whom insufficient evidence is held to warrant placing in categories A, B or C'. The ASIO officer charged with drawing up the list noted that the figure of sixty-three persons 'appears to be disproportionately higher' and explained that 'a considerable number of those recorded fall into category D, many of such having come under notice solely because of the manifestations of their advocacy of free thought'.[40]

Universities faced pressure from the government on more than one front. In addition to political pressure and moral and legal pressure to comply with the strictures of the intelligence services, financial pressure was applied. In some cases, this pressure was subtle and unspoken, but in others it was quite explicit – as in April 1951, when the Tasmanian government threatened to cut off state university funding if it didn't deal with the 'reds'.[41]

The dangers to academic freedom and university autonomy posed by universities' reliance on government funding were well understood by some critics, both inside and outside the academy. In 1956, Victorian Labor MP Jim Cairns pressed for an investigation into the financial needs of universities, with the goal of providing them with a 'more secure and autonomous footing'.[42] In the same year, the chancellor of the University of Melbourne, Charles Lowe, advocated for the establishment of an independent university grants committee to select outstanding researchers while minimising the risk that governments might interfere with university funding on political grounds.

The idea of a university grants committee resurfaced at the Commonwealth level in 1957, when the Committee on Australian Universities was appointed by Prime Minister Menzies. The committee was chaired by Sir Keith Murray, who also chaired the British University Grants Committee.[43] Its report, which was presented to the prime minister in September 1957, recommended that a university grants committee be established in Australia to administer Commonwealth grants to universities. It also recommended that the committee play an informal and advisory role.[44] Menzies didn't take this last bit of advice. He instead established a statutory commission that was empowered to 'coordinate the work of the universities'.[45]

Universities' Treatment of Dissident Academics

Some university leaders were complicit in facilitating the campaign against communism in universities, but others remained advocates of academic freedom and autonomy despite the considerable pressures they faced. At the University of Melbourne, the vice-chancellor John Medley unapologetically defended academic freedom and publicly confronted 'red hunters', vehemently maintaining that the university's role was to encourage free discussion and intelligent opposition.[46] In 1951, in response to allegations of left-wing propaganda and bias in university classrooms, the retiring vice-chancellor penned a letter to *The Age* which is worth quoting at some length for its contemporary resonance:

It is perfectly true that members of our staff occasionally are critical in public of government policy – whatever complexion that government may affect. I can see no reason why the rights of every citizen in a democracy should be denied.

It is true that the most talkative among our students are apt to favour extreme views – though at the present time the political color of 90 per cent of the members of the Students' Representative Council would be a grave disappointment to Mr. Stalin.

Intelligent youth is prone by nature to doubt, and there has never been so much food for doubt as there is at present.

If we mean anything by the assertion that we believe in democracy it is our duty to make it work; and the way to make it work is to encourage intelligent opposition.

The role of the university is to be a hotbed of discussion and thereby to train some of those who will someday provide that intelligent opposition, and intelligent government as well.

Freest possible discussion is the only way a university can do its job.

In present circumstances communism will and should figure largely in such discussions, and in the heat of youthful controversy labels will fly through the air and become attached to individuals, irrespective of the facts.

Fear of ideas never made a democratic community, and if we encourage it we are denying the very basis of our creed.[47]

That university leadership was often less robust in its defence of dissent and debate is illustrated by the case of Professor John Anderson, who was censured by the University of Sydney in the early 1930s.

Hailing from Scotland, Anderson was Sydney University's Challis Professor of Philosophy from 1927 to 1958 and the founder of its Freethought Society (which became the Libertarian Society in the 1950s). Anderson was described by admirers as 'the most original philosopher ever to have worked in Australia', and he was well known for controversial statements that were 'not fully comprehended by those who took exception to them'.[48]

Anderson's views were certainly provocative. On 9 July 1931, he delivered a lunchtime talk on patriotism to the Freethought Society. In the course of his talk he attacked 'various patriotic shibboleths as obscurantist' and criticised the role of war memorials in sanctifying war, describing the 'idols' and the rituals celebrating them as 'superstitious notions'.[49] According to *The Sydney Morning Herald*, which reported the event, Anderson also made remarks to the effect that Australia's 'political conditions could not be described as democratic', that the 'state of the country was a dictatorship', and that in Australia it 'was possible to arrest anyone who did not belong to the property class'. If the matters he chose to publicly discuss were 'opposed to existing laws and constitutions', he said, 'then these laws and constitutions must be wrong'.[50]

Anderson's comments were met with outrage from all directions: 'The local press ... erupted. Many state parliamentarians condemned him and the senate of the university censured him.'[51] As *The Brisbane Courier* reported, Anderson was asked 'to abstain from such utterances in the future'.[52] But Anderson was 'unrepentant' and defended himself before the senate:[53]

> The fight for freedom of thought and speech does not stop; it goes on. I have done nothing deserving of censure. I have stood for full discussion of important questions, which is an entirely academic thing to do. If I am not to oppose official views, this is not free speech. And until all members of the staff have been given a list of things they are not to say, they are serving under an unstated condition. The censure, I contend, ought to be withdrawn.[54]

His students also came to his defence, disputing claims that he taught them atheism, disloyalty and communist doctrine.[55]

More than ten years after being censured, Anderson was at the centre of another controversy. In 1943, he delivered an address to the New Education Fellowship as part of a lecture series on religion and education. Anderson's statements, which on this occasion were on the incompatibility of religion and education, once again generated outrage. This time around, however, the University of Sydney's reaction was more muted. Although the state parliament and the public urged the university senate to take action against Anderson, it refused to do so.[56] 'Possibly its failure twelve years earlier to restrain him made its members reluctant to try again,' speculates W.M. O'Neil, a colleague of Anderson's. But 'whatever the reason,' he concludes, 'it was an important assertion of university autonomy.'[57]

This episode represents a relatively modest case of interference with academic freedom; it is a far step from the more serious restrictions discussed later in this chapter. The pressure on the university to respond to Anderson's statements led to a relatively toothless censure in one instance and no action at all in the second. Yet a restriction it undoubtedly was and the failure of university authorities to stand for Professor Anderson's right to speak may well have helped to silence some who held similarly controversial views but had less strident personalities. Moreover, as Anderson's response to the censure indicates, such reprisals, which enforce 'unstated' restrictions on free speech, are apt to leave all academics unclear as to the limits of what they can say – a condition that is likely to give rise to self-censorship.

***

Scholars were perhaps most vulnerable to political prejudice when seeking employment. As we mentioned earlier, the rationales of selection committees were rarely transparent, but clear cases of academic candidates being turned down due to their political beliefs exist.

The treatment of Dr Thomas Kaiser is one such case. Kaiser was a distinguished physicist, and also a member of the Communist Party of Australia.[58] When he applied to be chair of physics at the University of New England in 1954, the selection committee assessed him as having 'the most brilliant future of any candidate' but doubted his suitability for the position 'in view of past political activities'.[59] As Cold War–historian Phillip Deery notes, Kaiser continued to have trouble finding employment in Australia, unsuccessfully applying for some thirty-three positions before departing for England 'to commence an illustrious career'.[60]

A more ambiguous case is that of Australian historian Russel Braddock Ward. Ward, who had been a member of the Communist Party until 1949, was unable to find an academic position in the mid-1950s, 'despite his evident talent and the near completion of his seminal and celebrated doctorate'.[61] In 1955, a selection committee recommended Ward for a lectureship at Sydney University of Technology (now the University of New South Wales), but he was told in January 1956 that the job would be readvertised.[62] The reasons given for the university's refusal to grant Ward the lectureship were contested at the time and still are. Max Hartwell, who was then the dean of humanities and chair of the selection committee, claimed that the vice-chancellor's decision was made on the basis of Ward's political leanings,[63] but the vice-chancellor, Philip Baxter, denied the university had applied a political or security test.[64] According to historian Frank Crowley, Baxter told him in conversation that Ward didn't get the job because of his 'questionable conduct' towards female school students while a schoolteacher,[65] but this claim is disputed by other historians.[66]

If Baxter's decision *was* politically motivated, how he learnt of Ward's former affiliation with the Communist Party is unknown. Fay Anderson writes that the vice-chancellor was informed of Ward's alleged activities in 'seditious circles' by the chair of the Public Service Board, Wallace Wurth.[67] Phillip Deery argues that Prime Minister Menzies' comments to parliament suggest the New South Wales Police Special Branch was responsible for sharing the information, despite the denials of the ASIO director-general.'[68]

Ward was eventually offered a history lectureship at the University of New England in 1957, and went on to serve as the university's deputy chancellor from 1981 to 1989.[69] If politics interfered with his early academic opportunities, it did not prevent him from ultimately having a successful career in Australia.

*

The dangers of being labelled a communist and the relative ease with which this could occur, even before the Cold War era started in earnest, are illustrated by the case of historian Raymond Maxwell Crawford, who, after a lectureship at the University of Sydney, was appointed chair in history at the University of Melbourne in 1936 and went on to become one of the leading historians of his time.

Crawford also served as vice-president of the Australian Council for Civil Liberties from 1938 to 1945 and was known for his public advocacy.[70] In May 1940, Crawford and thirty of his colleagues wrote a letter to the press criticising a regulation that limited the wartime reporting of communist and trade union newspapers.[71] Fellow members of Crawford's professorial board strongly objected to the fact that signatories of the letter noted their affiliation with the university.[72] Crawford defended himself before the board, arguing that he shouldn't be reprimanded for noting his affiliation with the university, because universities had 'a professional interest' in preserving freedom of expression.[73]

What followed shows how actively the political arm of government was engaged with the question of academics' political leanings and activities. Although Crawford had distanced himself from communism, he had retained the interest of the state government. In 1946, he was named in the Victorian parliament as a 'pink professor',[74] and in March the following year he was attacked by F.L. Edmunds, Liberal member for Hawthorn in the state legislative assembly, who had been invited by the University of Melbourne Liberal Club to deliver a lunchtime lecture on 'The Fight for World Supremacy'.[75] In front of an estimated 900 students, Edmunds voiced his displeasure with Crawford's perceived communist affiliations: 'It is a disgrace to the university that such a brilliant man as Professor Crawford should be associated with Australia-Soviet House, a communist subsidiary.'[76]

Crawford denied the accusations made against him:

> As to my being either a communist or a 'fellow traveller' with the communists, I must emphatically deny this. My differences with the Communist Party and doctrine are fundamental. If this were not so, I should not be afraid to avow it, and so long as I taught with integrity and objectivity, I should defend my right to hold unpopular opinion. But it is not so.[77]

His denial was a principled one, in that it defended the right of academics to have unpopular views, including communist beliefs. His defence of the left-wing press's right to publish was likewise principled, especially given his claims that he did not espouse their views. Yet the fact he felt the need to publicly refute such claims is telling: being branded a communist sympathiser was serious. As Fay Anderson puts it, 'For Crawford to have found it necessary to engage in such a debate reveals the changing political mood and his predisposition to deny any hint of public suspicion.'[78]

*

Other, less high-profile, cases demonstrate the difficulties experienced by academics who were left-wing or perceived to be so during this time. Physicist Dr Richard Makinson, a member of the Communist Party, was continually denied promotion by the University of Sydney due to his security record.[79] The appointment of Dutch economist Y.S. Brenner at the University of New South Wales was blocked by the vice-chancellor despite his being the selection committee's preferred candidate.[80] His subsequent application to the University of Adelaide was successful, but he was prevented from entering the country to take up the position.[81]

Anti-communist sentiment created the conditions for government and intelligence services to interfere with the workings of universities in Australia in ways that were clear intrusions into academic freedom and the right to freedom of speech about politics of university staff and students. In only a handful of cases can a clear line be drawn between the views espoused by academics and detriment to their careers. But those few cases, as well as the more ambiguous ones, had a chilling effect on academics who were critical of the government status quo, as did the atmosphere of suspicion created by public hostility and reports of students and faculty informing on other members of the academic community.

The Protest Era

In the 1960s and '70s, universities once again became centres of political and cultural change, attracting a new wave of criticism and concern from the government and the general public. While academics were most commonly the target of anti-communist discrimination in universities during the Cold War era, during this period the focus was often on students. That being said, academics were not immune from the criticism of both radical students and conservative governments.

Student protests and activism in Australia were part of a student protest movement that manifested itself in many different parts of the world. It may have peaked in 1968: that year alone witnessed the student-initiated general strike that paralysed Paris (commonly known as the May '68 revolution) and the large-scale student demonstrations in Mexico City, against authoritarianism and violations of university autonomy, which culminated in the Tlatelolco massacre, and the Columbia University anti-war and anti-segregation protests in New York City. University campuses during the 1960s have been described as the 'social base' of the era's 'challenge to the established order', and students as its 'moral, intellectual and administrative leadership'.[82]

In contrast to their more radical counterparts overseas, Australian students were relatively sedate in the late 1960s. *The Bulletin* observed as much in July 1968: 'After reading headlined accounts of violent student action in other part of the world this year, Australians have been inclined to think, Thank goodness our students aren't like that.'[83] However, the same article went on to sound a warning against complacency, citing a spate of recent student protests across the country. These included a civil rights march through the streets of Brisbane by students from the University of Queensland, a sit-in at the offices of the Commonwealth Department of National Services in Sydney, mass meetings at Monash University and the University of New South Wales demanding a say for students in university management, a protest outside Adelaide's Parliament House by the Students for Democratic Action and a march in Perth.[84] Australian students had concerns similar to those of students overseas, and they were responding with similar tactics, if not on the same scale or with the same intensity.

By the early 1970s, student unrest had intensified and the media was proclaiming that it was a time of 'crisis' for universities.[85] There were calls for university leaders and the government to intervene.

*

The factors that caused the blossoming of an unprecedented student movement in the late 1960s and early 1970s were the subject of much scholarly and public debate:[86]

No American or Australian student activity had ever been so militant, so sustained and so blatantly outside of the established organisations (including the communist parties) and institutions. Youth as a whole seemed to be in rebellion against the ways of the old. And this from a generation which was arguably the most affluent and healthy of all time. It simply didn't make sense.[87]

There were those who thought that the protests were unjustified and laid the blame on various inadequacies they perceived in the students and their generation. They were criticised as affluent and irresponsible or, as *The Age* described them in 1969, 'little more than a self-pitying coterie working out the aggression of their delayed adolescence'.[88] Some critics pointed to the permissive parenting style of the 1950s and 1960s, arguing that this created a cadre of 'psychologically maladjusted' young people.[89]

University Governance

Universities themselves did not escape students' scrutiny. Changes to the structure and functioning of universities – and in some cases their failure to change with the times – were met with a list of criticisms that may look familiar today. John Searle, a

University of California professor and administrator during this period, argues that student unrest could be traced to a number of issues at the institutional level, including increased student enrolment, the changing role of the university (he claims it began to function as a 'service station'), obsolete systems of university governance and assessment, and a crisis in educational philosophy (universities were transitioning away from the Renaissance ideal of the polymath and towards a model of specialisation).[90]

The structure and governance of universities were certainly not keeping pace with the expanding and increasingly diverse student population produced by the postwar boom.[91] Throughout the 1960s and 1970s, in Australia and overseas, students demanded to participate in university governance.[92] Students viewed administrators as the enemy and 'symptomatic of the wider refusals of autonomy' that their generation opposed.[93] They chafed against universities' bureaucratisation, declining teaching standards (universities were increasingly reliant on junior staff) and paternalistic attitudes towards students.[94]

Flashpoints arose from seemingly innocuous incidents, as a 1967 incident at the University of Sydney, now known as the Humphreys Affair, demonstrates. The incident began as a minor dispute: when the university raised library fines without consulting students, Student Action for the Rights of Students (SARS), an organisation led by postgraduate student Max Humphreys, responded by organising petitions and seeking to meet with university authorities on the matter. When the university refused to discuss the issue, SARS commenced a library sit-in on the evening of 6 April, with a list of grievances that now included 'the fining system, consultation with students and student participation in university decision making'.[95] The following morning, Humphreys was distributing invitations to a mass meeting to discuss further sit-ins when he was arrested by university police and charged with 'showing gross contempt of authority and inciting others to do the same'.[96]

A meeting of the proctorial board, which contained no student representation and gave the accused a limited right of reply, found Humphreys guilty and suspended him for a year.[97] Following his suspension, students mobilised a campaign on the issues of free speech and the university's disciplinary processes, culminating in a thousand students marching on the vice-chancellor's office on 14 April 1967. Just over a week later, the proctorial board met again and reversed its decision.[98]

Students at Monash University achieved similar success with direct action in May 1968. As reported by *The Age*, the leadership of Monash was considering revisions to its discipline statute, which would give it the power to punish students for misconduct committed outside the university's precincts.[99] A draft of the revised statute was expected to be accepted by the disciplinary committee that month before being put before the professorial board and then the University Council. This development was met with opposition from the student body. At a campus meeting attended by two thousand students, four motions were passed. Students demanded that the authorities 'take cognisance of student objects', that students 'not be subjected to university discipline for private activities off campus' and that students compose 'at least 50% of the membership of the discipline committee in the future'. They also stated that were the university to move ahead with adopting the regulations, students would 'not accept their power to do so'.[100] Mirroring the tactics of the 1964 Free Speech Movement at the University of California, Berkeley, and the 1967 anti-war and anti-segregation protests at Columbia University, Monash students occupied the administration building.[101] By June, the University Council had passed a resolution, accepting 'in principle the view that in general students should not be disciplined by the university for private activities off campus'.[102]

Right across Australia, students were demanding a say in the decision-making processes of their universities, and they were determined to be heard, even by those on the highest rungs of power. Robert Menzies discovered this when he was harangued by a group of fifty student protesters outside a special meeting of the Council of the University of Melbourne in July 1969. According to *The Sun,* his 'usual delight in a verbal tussle seemed to be missing'. When the students told him they were seeking greater access to meetings and asked if he would discuss the matter with them, he reportedly responded, '"Certainly not" ... with a wave of his hand.'[103]

Following the election of Prime Minister Gough Whitlam in December 1972, and the end of twenty years of conservative federal leadership, student activism intensified, rather than abated.[104] Over time, sustained student protests led to the inclusion of student representatives on various governing, policy and disciplinary bodies, which has been maintained to this day, but not the radically democratic reformation for which some students agitated.

Vietnam War and Conscription

The students of the 1960s and '70s were protesting more than just the university system and its issues. They were tapping into a sense of dissatisfaction with the established order of broader society.[105] In Australia, students had come to articulate the hopes and frustrations of an expanding middle class, which, as 'the old prewar elites held on to power by Menzies' coat-tails', was impatient for change.[106] The first generation for whom television and international travel were generally accessible, they were more aware of political and cultural causes being championed elsewhere in the world.[107] Within this broader context of progressive possibility, particular issues became rallying points for student activists (and many non-student activists), leading the government and some sections of the public to criticise both students and the universities they attended.

Of all the diverse issues that Australian students rallied around, the most politically salient was conscription for the Vietnam War – doubtless, in part, because of the very immediate impact it had on so many young men of that generation. Under the *National Service Act 1964*, all twenty-year-old males were required to register with the Department of Labour and National Service, and were selected via 'birthday ballot'. In May 1968, a Bill introduced by the Gorton government provided two years' jail for draft resisters, sparking student-led demonstrations in support of conscientious objectors.[108] As historian Russell Marks argues, it was the fact of conscription, more than any other issue, that 'underpinned the radicalism of middle-class university students' during this period.[109]

Menzies' announcement in April 1965 that servicemen would be sent to Vietnam sparked further protests, which notably included a sit-in demonstration at the Australian Student Labour Federation Conference in Canberra 1965, and another in Sydney, at which fifty-one students were arrested.[110]

Students demonstrated against the Coalition leading up to the federal election of 1966, which turned on the issues of the Vietnam War and conscription. The fact that Labor lost nine seats in the election shook the faith that many student protesters had in the parliamentary democratic system and contributed to a radicalisation of their views and methods.[111] Activism that had focused on pacifism and anti-racism shifted to encompass attacks on 'mainstream culture and the existing political system'.[112]

In the late 1960s, some student groups began advocating for the National Liberation Front of South Vietnam (NLF). Their advocacy included voicing moral support (the Australian Student Labor Federation), raising funds for medical aid (the Labor clubs at the University of Sydney) and raising funds for unspecified support (the Monash University Labor Club).[113] These efforts were condemned as treasonous by the government, the mainstream media, the RSL and even by some members of the Labor Party.[114] On campus, they also attracted opposition from other students. At Monash, groups of right-wing students responded with violence, with small groups – 'some emblazoned with swastikas' – physically attacking members of the Labor Club.[115] Monash University's acting vice-chancellor, Professor R.R. Andrew, had a balanced response to the students' fundraising efforts: he ordered that no collections be made for the NLF on campus but allowed contributions for medical aid to be made through a London doctor's committee, and he personally donated to the fund, which some saw as 'a gesture to mitigate the severity of his actions'.[116] The federal government later responded with the introduction of the *Defence Force Protection Act 1967,* making it a crime to send aid to the North Vietnam government or the NLF, punishable by two years' imprisonment and/or a fine of $2000.[117]

On 11 April 1969, there was a national day of action against conscription and the Vietnam War. In Adelaide, some four hundred students assembled at the Barr Smith Lawns before marching on to the Labour and

National Service building, where around eighty students proceeded to occupy a corridor on the second floor.[118] Police attempts to evict the protesters turned violent, and there were conflicting reports of the event: 'The local dailies came out with their mandatory stories about violent student protestors and there were calls for the universities to keep their students in check'.[119] Flinders University's vice-chancellor, Professor Peter Karmel, had a liberal response. At a degree-conferring ceremony a few days after the day of action, he acknowledged student concerns about the issues of Vietnam and university governance and their right to express them:

> Groups of students have made their views known, have protested, have demonstrated ... [While I] disagree with some of the views expressed and methods used, I cannot but approve of the active interest of students, for it is precisely this sort of interest that a university education ought to stimulate.[120]

However, the vice-chancellor also defended the right of the university to remain neutral on these issues and to foster an environment that enabled rational debate:

> The university should not be an active agent for a particular set of values embodied in a particular program for society. To do that would, in my opinion, destroy the university in its essential elements. The value for which the university stands, the value which is inherent in the nature of the university, is a belief in free, critical and rational enquiry. This cannot take place in an atmosphere of emotion and prejudice, nor can it take place in an atmosphere of physical or verbal violence. Consequently, we must preserve in the university an environment in which discussions can be conducted calmly and in which opposing views, however hardly argued, are listened to. And we must protect the right to dissent. Moreover, the university must be prepared to fight any threat to free, critical and rational

enquiry within the university, whether the threats comes from within the university or from without.[121]

The violence that sometimes occurred during student protests continued to present problems for universities. Whenever protests took a violent turn, as did a demonstration outside the US consulate in Melbourne on 4 July 1968, it fuelled conservatives' claims that protesters threatened the social order and scandalised university alumni, who urged their alma maters to take action.[122] State governments also expressed their dissatisfaction. Responding to student occupations of the University of Sydney campus in April 1969, Premier Robert Askin issued universities with a warning: discipline offending students or don't 'expect my government to look sympathetically' at funding requests.[123]

*

Mass street marches began to occur in Australian cities in the early 1970s. On 8 May 1970, up to a hundred thousand people marched through the streets of Melbourne to protest the Vietnam War.[124] The march included many members of the university community. One attendee, a student at the University of Melbourne and member of its regiment explained the significance of the march:

> Fully 5000 Melbourne Uni staff and students marched against the war and the draft that day, well over a third of the total full-time enrolment. When we finally reached the city, a gigantic crowd dwarfed even the largest hope ... The papers said as previously. Gaily we called out to the shoppers and office workers to join us and many did. The war rolled on as we sat in the street and listened to the speeches, but we felt that we were fulfilled.[125]

The public perception of Australia's involvement in the Vietnam War began to change. While opposition to the war was initially met with hostility and seen as evidence of student radicalism, the tide shifted and the anti-war movement became more mainstream. The organisational skills and nonconfrontational tactics of the moratorium movement came to be particularly well-regarded. The movement received positive coverage in newspapers and was interpreted as evidence that the anti-war movement had 'come of age'.[126] In his history of protest in Australia, Clive Hamilton describes the power of the moratorium protests:

> Across Australia, some 200,000 marched, in big cities and small towns alike, and it was apparent even to the war's staunchest advocates that their cause was lost. The media, which has been dismissive or hostile of the protests, began to criticise the war.[127]

The shift in public sentiment had an impact on mainstream politics, leading to a change in Labor Party policy with respect to Australian involvement in Vietnam. On 1 October 1969, federal Labor leader Gough Whitlam delivered an election policy speech promising that, 'under Labor, there [would] be no Australian troops left in Vietnam after June 1970'.[128] While Labor didn't go on to win that election, the withdrawal of Australian forces from Vietnam began in 1970 anyway, likely as a result of public pressure. When the Whitlam government came to power two years later, the last of the troops were brought home.

Systemic Racism

While protests against the Vietnam War and conscription attracted the most focus from the media and drew the largest crowds, the student movement of the 1960s and 1970s had a wider range of concerns. Prominent among these was the rejection of racist policy both in Australia and overseas.

When Prime Minister Robert Menzies described South Africa's apartheid regime as a domestic matter in 1960, thousands of students demonstrated in Sydney's Martin Place.[129] The police responded violently, solidifying a common conviction among student protesters that the state was a not a neutral actor in these matters.[130] The University of Sydney's student newspaper, *Honi Soit,* drew attention to the police response and called for donations to help those arrested pay their fines.[131]

In 1961, a student action group was formed at the University of Melbourne to advocate for moral issues such as the abolition of the White Australia policy to be put on the agenda for the upcoming federal election. Members of the group attended and interrupted the campaign events of Labor leader Arthur Calwell and Prime Minister Robert Menzies by yelling anti-racist slogans.[132]

In May 1964, students protested outside the US consulate in Sydney in support of the American civil-rights movement. International media reported the protests, but highlighted the irony of Australian students demonstrating against racism in the United States when the White Australia policy was still in place and discrimination against Indigenous people widespread.[133]

Soon afterwards, Student Action for Aborigines (SAFA) was formed, led by Aboriginal activist and Sydney University student Charles Perkins (who went on to become secretary of the Department of Aboriginal Affairs in 1981). The following year, inspired by the freedom rides of the American civil-rights movement, Perkins and thirty-three other SAFA members set off on a bus tour of country towns in northern New South Wales to bring attention to racial segregation.[134] The tour was reported by news outlets around the world, which chronicled the hostility, abuse and even violence the activists were met with:

> The students have been pelted with gravel in their trip from small town to small town, heckled and pushed by white crowds, barred from staying in a church hall, and locked out of a segregated movie house. Their bus has been forced off the road by angry white [drivers]. Their first driver quit, saying the job was too dangerous. The new driver is not sure how long he will serve.[135]

The freedom rides focused media attention on the significant discrimination experienced by Indigenous people around Australia and emboldened a new generation of activists.[136] Although they are just one part of a long history of Indigenous-rights activism, they played a big role in bringing about the 1967 referendum and getting it passed. The referendum removed barriers to including Indigenous people in national censuses and granted the Commonwealth the power to expand Indigenous rights, which were previously determined at a state and territory level. Its passing was greeted as a significant symbolic victory for Indigenous rights and reconciliation. The impact the 1965 Freedom Ride had on the Australian political landscape is difficult to overstate. In the words of historian and former SAFA member Ann Curthoys, it was an essential contribution to 'the moral formation of a generation'.[137]

The Perspective of History

Our brief overview of some of the more tumultuous and challenging periods in the history of Australian universities provides a context for understanding today's debates about academic freedom and on-campus free speech. In the past, government often posed a far more significant threat to academic freedom and free speech than politically dissident academics or periodic bouts of student disruption and protest. While nowhere near as pernicious as the actions of the US government during the McCarthy era, the Menzies government's direct interference in university matters during the Cold War was arguably the lowest point for academic freedom in Australia.

In the light of this history, recent calls for the government to take an active role in monitoring free speech on Australian campuses and to interfere with the autonomy of our universities should be treated with caution. Such interventions have the potential to undermine the very freedoms they are claiming to protect. If the justification for such interference is that we are now witnessing an unprecedented crisis of free speech on Australian campuses – a crisis created by politically intolerant students and faculty – it is not a justification informed by any serious consideration of the history.

This narrative should also lead us to reconsider how university students and their behaviour is understood. In his study of universities in the United Kingdom, Evan Smith locates the origins of the current debate on free speech in universities – particularly claims that radical leftist students censor the opinions of conservatives – in a culture war dating back to the 1960s.[138] Smith argues that the stereotype of students as 'far-left provocateurs' who are 'subversive, dangerous and potentially violent' became prominent alongside the growth of the student movements of the late 1960s and early '70s.[139] Protests against conservative politicians and other speakers (such as Conservative Party politician Enoch Powell in 1968) led to accusations that students 'used intimidation to harangue speakers who put forward ideas they did not like' and didn't respect freedom of speech.[140]

In the following decade, he argues, the stereotype of the university student as 'over-sensitive and easily offended' emerged, a precursor to today's 'snowflake'.[141] During the 1990s, claims that political correctness was having a censoring effect were imported from the US culture wars.[142] Since that time, the right has largely characterised university students as so preoccupied with identity politics as to be a threat to freedom of speech.

Smith's analysis has obvious resonance in Australian universities, given their cultural and political connections to the United Kingdom. A circular pattern is discernible here. The students of the 1960s and '70s were condemned for their radicalism, which their critics ascribed to generational failings, poor parenting and psychological immaturity, among other things. Yet, in their later years, members of that same generation proved they were themselves prepared to make similar accusations against the generations that came after them.

It is salutary to remember that positions that once appeared radical and agendas that were in the past dismissed as the political lunacy of students are now accepted as common sense. There are no supporters of apartheid or racial segregation in the modern political mainstream, yet when protesters first challenged the policies that underpinned these systems, their views were deeply divisive and their politics marginal.

In terms of university protests, the last decade has been relatively quiet, and the recent Independent Review chaired by the Honourable Robert French explicitly rejected the notion that there is a free speech crisis in Australian universities.[143] If anything, today's students are less radical and politicised than their predecessors. While the magnifying power of social media amplifies controversial events, the number of speakers at Australian universities who have faced protests is dwarfed by the huge number of speakers who have not. Speakers who have been successfully prevented from speaking are fewer still. The violence of student action in earlier decades has only a very pale reflection today.

2

LAWS AND REGULATIONS PROTECTING ACADEMIC FREEDOM AND FREEDOM OF SPEECH

Our focus in this chapter is on the obligations of universities in relation to academic freedom and free speech in Australia. In the period leading up to the Independent Review headed by the Honourable Robert French in 2019, universities came in for some criticism on this subject, with certain critics erroneously claiming there was widespread failure on the part of universities to meet their statutory obligations.[1]

As we show, however, any claim that universities were failing to meet their obligations prior to the Independent Review is likely based on one of two mistaken assumptions: that the concept of intellectual freedom encompasses freedom of speech, or that universities are mandated to have a standalone policy on free intellectual inquiry under section 19.115 of the *Higher Education Support Act.*[2] The latter assumption is particularly poorly founded, there being no mention of a 'standalone' policy in the Act and very little indication – anywhere in the regulatory scheme – as to exactly what policy response is required of universities.

Universities typically *had* been providing for protection of academic freedom before the Independent Review commenced, although their protection of free speech on university campuses was patchier. With this in mind, we examine the recommendations of the Independent Review in relation to the protection of freedom of speech and academic freedom in other countries. We also review the way that Australian universities have so far responded to the Independent Review.

Commonwealth Legislation
The Higher Education Support Act

The centrepiece of Australian law on academic freedom is section 19.115 of the *Higher Education Support Act.* It requires that both public and private universities 'have a policy that upholds free intellectual inquiry in relation to learning, teaching and research' as a condition of receiving government funding. This requirement was introduced as an amendment to the Act in 2011, as part of a broader package of higher education reforms.[3]

The general policy concerns that gave rise to the amendment are evident from the 2011 Bill's explanatory memorandum, which recognises that 'free intellectual inquiry is an important principle underpinning the provision of higher education in Australia'.[4] There was no indication that the government felt it was responding to any kind of crisis in the sector by introducing the Bill. When then education minister Peter

Garrett commented on the Bill at its second reading in Parliament, he recognised that most universities already had adequate policies in place and 'wish[ed] to support research and teaching environments which promote free intellectual inquiry'.[5] The main concern he expressed was that the conditionality of government funding 'should not be used to impede free intellectual inquiry'.[6]

TEQSA and the Threshold Standards

The Tertiary Education Quality and Standards Agency (TEQSA) is the quality assurance and regulatory agency for the higher education sector. TEQSA was established by the *Tertiary Education Quality and Standards Agency Act 2011* and its functions are guided by the Higher Education Standards Framework (Threshold Standards) 2015. The Threshold Standards set the minimum level of achievement a higher education provider must meet and maintain in order to operate as a registered provider, and also detail a provider's obligations, including its obligation to uphold free intellectual inquiry.

The duty to uphold free intellectual inquiry is enunciated under standard 6.1.4 ('Corporate Governance'). Notably, the standard sits this duty alongside several others:

> The governing body [must take] steps to develop and maintain an institutional environment in which freedom of intellectual inquiry is upheld and protected, students and staff are treated equitably, the wellbeing of students and staff is fostered, informed decision-making by students is supported and students have opportunities to participate in the deliberative and decision making-processes of the higher education provider.[7]

Presumably, if any of these requirements were to conflict with each other, the higher education provider would need to strike a balance in order to satisfy the overall requirement of providing a suitable institutional environment for staff and students.

Other duties detailed in the Threshold Standards (some of which overlap with those cited in standard 6.1.4) may also affect the way a provider responds to issues of free intellectual inquiry. One such duty is the provision of a diverse and equitable learning environment:

Institutional policies, practices and approaches to teaching [must be] designed to accommodate student diversity, including the under-representation and/or disadvantage experienced by identified groups, and create equivalent opportunities for academic success regardless of students' backgrounds.[8]

Another is the provision of a learning environment that promotes the wellbeing and safety of students:

[A] safe environment [must be] promoted and fostered, including by advising students and staff on actions they can take to enhance safety and security on campus and online'.

The Threshold Standards thus introduce a range of conditions that a higher education provider must satisfy. Although these conditions are often compatible, at times they will be in tension with one another.[9] When free intellectual inquiry is found to conflict with the value of equity, diversity, wellbeing or safety, this conflict may be at the centre of a dispute related to free speech or academic freedom. The difficult task of reconciling and balancing these values is discussed in chapters 3 and 4.

TEQSA Guidance Notes

Some indication of how a university's duty to protect free intellectual inquiry is meant to interact with its duty to uphold other essential values can be found in TEQSA's Guidance Notes for the Higher Education Standards Framework (Threshold Standards) 2015. The Guidance Notes are intended to 'provide greater clarity for providers in the interpretation and application of the selected standards', but it is important to note that they have no binding force and do not replace the Threshold Standards themselves.[10]

One important aspect of the Guidance Notes is the priority they give to free inquiry over the accommodation of diversity. The 'Diversity and Equity' guidance note affirms that universities are required to protect diversity:

> The Standards necessitate that providers have an understanding of the concepts of diversity and equity, and have considered the implications for their operations, including the creation of a culture that welcomes diversity (on campus and online)'.

But the same note also goes on to clearly state that free intellectual inquiry cannot be infringed as a result:

> Measures taken to accommodate diversity should also not contravene the pursuit of free intellectual inquiry and more generally, freedom of expression.[11]

Nonetheless, it is evident that the Guidance Notes envision a broad conception of wellbeing and safety that could be vulnerable to harmful speech, including online speech:

> [The Threshold Standards] includes a section on wellbeing and safety that requires providers to ... promote and foster a safe

environment on campus and online ... The terms 'wellbeing' and 'safety' are used in their ordinary meanings, broadly encompassing 'overall wellness' and 'freedom from harm' respectively.[12]

The broad definition afforded to 'wellbeing' and 'safety' – together with the application of standard 2.3 ('Wellbeing and Safety') to online forums, where harm is more likely to be speech-based – suggests that universities *do* have a duty to protect their communities from the harm that may arise from free speech or other expressive conduct. However, no mechanisms for addressing such harm are specified.[13]

The Meaning of 'Free Intellectual Inquiry'

The concept of free intellectual inquiry is at the centre of the regulatory framework for higher education. But despite that centrality, neither the *Higher Education Support Act,* the *TEQSA Act* nor the Threshold Standards provide a definition of its meaning. It appears, however, to be close to the idea of academic freedom: the freedom and privilege of academics (and sometimes others) to carry out research, publication and teaching activities.[14] The *Higher Education Support Act,* for example, specifies that the policy upholding free intellectual inquiry relates to 'learning, teaching and research' – in other words, academic activities.

Garrett's statement in the second reading of the 2011 Higher Education Support Amendment confirms that 'free intellectual inquiry' covers academic activity:

It is fundamental to the scientific method and rigorous scholarship. It is necessary to enable evidence to be challenged, competing theories to be debated and facts to be established. It provides the foundation for our understanding of the world and the accumulation of knowledge.[15]

However, some confusion seems to have arisen later. The chief commissioner of TEQSA, Professor Nicholas Saunders, has indicated the agency has a broader interpretation of free intellectual inquiry:

> We're thinking about freedom of expression, freedom of speech as well as freedom to actually investigate and teach those sorts of things.[16]

TEQSA's more capacious understanding of free intellectual inquiry has the advantage of recognising that universities have obligations beyond supporting academic activity. However, it does risk causing confusion between academic freedom and freedom of speech, which are often treated as synonymous but are in fact distinct. Some activity covered by academic freedom – conducting experiments or archival research, for example – is not obviously expressive. That activity would not be covered by a free speech principle, and neither would the institutional autonomy of universities, which is another aspect of academic freedom (we examine this further in chapters 3 and 5). By the same token, much activity on campus that comes under the principle of free speech – political protest, visiting speakers and the like – is not part of the teaching and research activities of the university and not the subject of academic freedom.

We think that much potential confusion could be avoided by adopting the recommendation of the 'Report of the Independent Review' to update the Threshold Standards and the *Higher Education Support Act* by replacing the term 'free intellectual inquiry' with 'freedom of speech and academic freedom' and introducing a definition of academic freedom.[17] The need for clarification along these lines is made especially evident by the full Federal Court's 2020 decision upholding the termination of Peter Ridd. The argument for Ridd relied upon the protection of 'intellectual freedom' in the James Cook University Enterprise Agreement 2013–2016. The Federal Court, however, insisted on a distinction between 'intellectual freedom' (as defined in the enterprise agreement) and 'academic freedom', and explicitly put to one side any substantive consideration of the idea of 'academic freedom'. The concept was, in their view, too uncertain to accord it any legal meaning.[18]

Some useful illustrations of how an amendment might be drafted are found in other jurisdictions. For instance, academic freedom is legally defined in New Zealand as follows:

a)   the freedom of academic staff and students, within the law, to question and test received wisdom, to put forward new ideas and to state controversial or unpopular opinions;

b)   the freedom of academic staff and students to engage in research;

c)   the freedom of the institution and its staff to regulate the subject matter of courses taught at the institution;

d)   the freedom of the institution and its staff to teach and assess students in the manner they consider best promotes learning;

e)   the freedom of the institution through its chief executive to appoint its own staff.[19]

Under this definition, academic freedom is a freedom held by the institution itself as well as by academic staff and students. It includes the freedom to express opinions within the law, to engage in research and to teach, assess and determine course content without interference. The concept of academic freedom in New Zealand is justified by the accepted role of universities 'as critic and conscience of society'.[20]

The protection of academic freedom in the United Kingdom's *Education Reform Act 1988* is sparser, but it also focuses on the core research and teaching activities of the university. Under this Act,[21] university regulators have a duty

> to ensure that academic staff have freedom within the law to question and test received wisdom, and to put forward new ideas and controversial or unpopular opinions, without placing themselves in jeopardy of losing their jobs or privileges they may have at their institutions.[22]

A 2011 report by representative organisation Universities UK elaborated on this idea.[23] Defining academic freedom much like New Zealand's

Education Act 1989, it associates academic freedom with the following values:

- freedom from state and political interference
- institutional self-governance and autonomy
- individual freedom to undertake teaching
- institutional excellence
- security of academic tenure
- peer review and open and rigorous criticism of ideas.[24]

Protection Provided by Universities before 2018

We turn now to consider the way Australian universities had met their statutory obligations to protect free intellectual inquiry prior to the Independent Review. The assessment is complicated by the lack of clarity in the regulatory framework. Because the central term 'free intellectual inquiry' is not defined, it is difficult to pinpoint exactly what universities are meant to protect. (Is it just academic activities? Or is it freedom of speech more generally?) There is also very little specificity as to what actions are required of universities with respect to enforcing these protections.

The assessment is complicated again by the varying legal authority of the mechanisms employed by universities to implement regulatory requirements. These mechanisms include enterprise agreements, which are legally binding and enforceable through the Fair Work Commission. However, if an enterprise agreement conflicts with Commonwealth legislation, it can be overruled. By contrast, university policies have different levels of legal authority depending on context: in some states and territories, universities are delegated lawmaking powers by parliament. Other university policies are enforceable only within the university. All university policies must respect the university's enterprise agreement.

Despite the diversity of these mechanisms, all Australian universities have long had some protection for academic freedom in place that at least partially fulfils their statutory obligations.

Some of these mechanisms have also extended to protect freedom of speech.

Institution-Specific Legislation

In certain cases, institution-specific enacting legislation, which sets out the objects, powers and functions of universities, makes reference to free intellectual inquiry. The *University of Melbourne Act 2009,* for example, states that one of the objects of the university is 'to serve the Victorian, Australian and international communities and the public interest by ... promoting critical and free inquiry, informed intellectual discourse and public debate within the university and in the wider society'.[25] It also requires that appointees to the University Council have 'an appreciation of the values of a university relating to teaching, research, independence and academic freedom'.[26]

Enterprise Agreements

Perhaps the most important mechanism for the legal protection of academic freedom is the enterprise agreement, which typically affirms the importance of academic freedom as a right of academic staff members.

One example is Central Queensland University Enterprise Agreement 2017, which states that the university and its staff 'recognise that guarantees of intellectual and academic freedom are essential to the proper functioning of a university culture'. It goes on to affirm that employees have the right to:

- pursue critical and open inquiry
- participate in public debates and express opinions about their discipline, general social issues and higher education issues
- participate in decision-making processes within the university via appropriate representation on university committees
- participate in professional and representative bodies, including trade unions, without fear of harassment or intimidation
- undertake all aspects of their role without fear or harassment, bullying, intimidation or unfair treatment.[27]

The same clause also emphasises that the right to academic freedom guaranteed to students and employees is linked to their responsibility 'to support the role of CQ University as a place of independent learning and thought, where ideas may be put forward and opinion expressed freely; and as an institution which must be accountable for its expenditure of public money, and which upholds the values of truth, accuracy, honesty, civility and courage'.[28]

Policies on Academic Freedom

Many universities have specific policies in place to support academic freedom, which are typically referred to as 'academic freedom policies' or 'intellectual freedom policies'. Together with university statements on academic freedom, these policies provide the most detailed explication of the concept of academic freedom, its justification and the actual protections it affords.

Like the enterprise agreement of Central Queensland University, most academic freedom policies recognise that academic freedom also entails responsibilities. The University of Melbourne's policy affirms that scholars at the university should not be disadvantaged or subject to less favourable treatment for exercising their academic freedom, but explicitly states that 'like all rights, the right to academic freedom of expression carries responsibilities'.[29] It notes that academic discourse should be undertaken reasonably and in good faith, and must comply with the principles of academic and research ethics, such as supporting an argument with reason. It suggests that scholars who choose to speak on an area outside of their expertise should consider whether it is reasonable for their comments to be associated with the university.

University statements and charters on academic freedom often also include a reference to the responsibilities of academic freedom. RMIT University's statement on academic freedom and responsibility provides a detailed summary of the role of the university community, the justifications for academic freedom and the responsibility of scholars to respect the principles of academic integrity and inclusivity:

Universities are important sites for the production and reproduction of knowledge. Universities are also places where free and open inquiry thrives and where systems of knowledge are critiqued and challenged. Claims and assertions are not taken at face value and cannot be based simply on emotion and personal belief; arguments must be substantiated by rigorous scholarship and supported by evidence.

In this context, RMIT University is a community of scholars and teachers united by the shared commitment to the value of research, education and scholarship for the practical betterment of humanity. Our intellectual community includes teachers, academics, researchers and students who span the vocational and higher education spectrum.

RMIT University upholds and protects the right of members of our community of scholars to be intellectually curious, to be forthright in the respectful expression of informed views and to be able to express their views free from undue institutional constraint.

Scholars exercising their right to academic freedom do so with an awareness of – and acceptance of – their responsibilities with respect to satisfying the principles of academic and research integrity, including declaring any relevant affiliations and potential conflicts of interest, and acknowledging the rights of others to express differing views.

RMIT University recognises that given their role in producing, re-producing and critiquing knowledge, members of our community of scholars often speak from positions of power and influence. Our commitment to being intellectually curious is founded on the inclusive principle that the advancement of knowledge is best achieved through active participation of marginalised groups.[30]

This version of the policy has since been replaced, but the new iteration also includes a statement about expectations and responsibilities, including the responsibility of staff to 'act in good faith, in accordance with their own professional judgement having due regard to the expectations of their discipline'.[31]

Other Policies

Other university policies also have a bearing on academic freedom and freedom of speech. These may include codes of conduct, research policies, public comment policies and social media policies. The University of Western Australia's code of conduct, for example, specifically includes academic freedom as part of its code on equity and justice:

Academic freedom is recognised and protected by this university as essential to the proper conduct of teaching, research and scholarship.

Freedom of intellectual thought and enquiry and the open exchange of ideas and evidence are a university core value. All academic and research staff should be guided by a commitment to freedom of inquiry and exercise their traditional rights to examine social values and to criticise and challenge the belief structures of society in the spirit of a responsible and honest search for knowledge and its dissemination. In this context students have the right to participate in political activities on campus.[32]

Its charter of student rights adds that students have the right 'to be able to communicate freely, to voice alternative points of view in rational debate, and to have their intellectual freedom protected'.[33]

Social media policies and research policies also address academic freedom and freedom of speech. Bond University's media policy affirms the university's commitment to academic freedom, and provides that 'members of the university community are free to contribute to public debate'.[34] Flinders

University's research policy states that the university will foster responsible research by 'actively encouraging mutual cooperation with open exchange of ideas between peers, and respect for freedom of expression and inquiry'.[35]

Protections for Freedom of Speech

Few universities have drawn a distinction between academic freedom and the broader right to freedom of speech. Consequently, separate and explicit references to freedom of speech are not as common in university policy. The definition of 'intellectual freedom' in Charles Darwin University's code of conduct is a good example of the way free speech and academic freedom are often conflated; it refers to article 19 of the Universal Declaration of Human Rights, which provides a definition of the right to free expression.[36]

More extensive and explicit protections for freedom of speech are provided in the University of Southern Queensland's code of conduct for students, which states that the university aims to provide an environment where 'freedom of expression is protected and encouraged' and requires students to 'consider their responsibilities and the consequences of their actions when exercising their freedom of expression' and to avoid impairing 'the rights of others to participate in any legitimate university activity'.[37] Similarly, the University of Melbourne's policy on student conduct requires students to 'respect the rights of other members of the university community to express dissent or different political or religious views, subject to those actions or views complying with the laws of Australia' and to 'respect the opinions of others and engage in rational debate in areas of disagreement'.[38]

More succinct statements in support of freedom of speech are found in a range of policies and charters across the sector. Monash University's ethics policy briefly states that it values 'freedom of thought and of expression'.[39] Curtin University's research management policy states that the responsible conduct of research involves the 'open exchange of ideas between peers, and respect for freedom of expression and inquiry'.[40] And the University of Canberra's conduct and values charter states that 'the university is traditionally a place where freedom of speech is respected, where free and open discussion and intellectual debate is encouraged'.[41]

The Independent Review

In November 2018, amid the claims of a 'free speech crisis' on university campuses, education minister Dan Tehan announced an independent review of the rules and regulations protecting free speech on university campuses. Robert French, a former chief justice of the High Court of Australia, was selected to lead the review, and he emphasised that it would be undertaken 'on a cooperative and consultative basis with the university sector' and with respect for 'the legitimate institutional autonomy of Australian universities'.[42] Tehan, who was clearly influenced by debates in the United States, foresaw that the review might 'lead to the development of an Australian version of the Chicago Statement, which is a voluntary framework that clearly sets out a university's commitment to promoting freedom of speech'. In line with these expectations, French agreed that the review would produce 'a model code which can be used as a point of reference in any consideration by universities of their existing rules and guidelines relating to the protection of freedom of speech on campus'.[43]

The Independent Review's terms of reference were to:

- assess the effectiveness of the Higher Education Standards Framework (the Standards) to promote and protect freedom of expression and freedom of intellectual inquiry in higher education;
- assess the effectiveness of the policies and practices to address the requirements of the Standards, to promote and protect freedom of expression and intellectual inquiry;
- assess international approaches to the promotion and protection of free expression and free intellectual

inquiry in higher education settings, and consider whether any of these approaches would add to protections already in place in the Australian context;

- outline realistic and practical options that could be considered to better promote and protect freedom of expression and freedom of intellectual inquiry, including:
  * revision/clarification of the Standards
  * development of a sector-led code of conduct.[44]

Findings and Recommendations

The three-hundred-page 'Report of the Independent Review of Freedom of Speech in Australian Higher Education Providers' was released on 6 April 2019. A summary of the report is provided in appendix A. One of the report's key findings is that there is no 'crisis' in freedom of speech on Australian campuses.[45] As French concludes, 'Reported incidents in Australia in recent times do not establish a systemic pattern of action by higher education providers or student representative bodies, adverse to freedom of speech or intellectual inquiry in the higher education sector.'[46] He also concedes, however, that a small number of incidents seen to be infringing freedom of speech 'may have an adverse impact on public perception of the higher education sector which can feed into the political sphere ... [and] may have a "chilling effect" on the exercise of freedom of speech in some places'.[47]

The report acknowledges that discussions about the limits of academic freedom and freedom of speech in universities are far from new, but concludes that the current debate is distinguishable by its focus on the following points of disagreement: (1) the appropriate response of universities to speech affecting 'social, cultural, ethnic and religious sensitivities' and 'vulnerable members of the staff and student communities'; (2) the role of scholarly standards in determining who can speak on campus; and (3) how to approach speech that may affect the university's reputation or its relationship with third parties (on this point, university administrators are likely to have different views to academics and students).[48]

The report observes that the diversity of the current array of university regulations and the generality of the language they use leaves too much room for the exercise of 'administrative discretion and evaluative judgments'. This discretion itself has the potential to undermine freedom of speech and academic freedom, and make 'the sector an easy target for criticism'.[49]

However, the report also acknowledges that such discretion is an important aspect of institutional autonomy, which, as French points out, is itself 'a dimension of academic freedom'. The solution, he argues, is not greater government regulation but clarification of the existing regulatory framework. With this goal in mind, the report recommends that references to 'free intellectual inquiry' be changed to 'freedom of speech and academic freedom' in the *Higher Education Support Act* and the Threshold

Standards, and that a definition for academic freedom be introduced to both.[50]

The report's principal recommendation is for universities to adopt umbrella principles on free speech and academic freedom, as part of a code of practice or model code. Adoption would be voluntary in order to maintain universities' institutional autonomy.[51] Ultimately, French does not recommend a statutory duty in relation to freedom of expression, suggesting that the policy implications of a new law went beyond the scope of review: 'The recommendation of a model code, operationalising umbrella principles, coupled with cognate amendments to the *HES Act [Higher Education Support Act 2003]* and the HE Standards [Threshold Standards] should be sufficient unto the day.'[52]

Responses

The process of responding to the report's recommendations is ongoing and all universities are taking action in a variety of ways. As Universities

Australia has pointed out, the task of synthesising the Model Code presented in the 'Report of the Independent Review' with universities' existing policies is complex.[53] Some universities have chosen to modify their pre-existing policies, some have elected to adopt new standalone policies of their own devising, and others have opted to implement the Model Code in an amended form.[54]

Critics have argued argued that the protections afforded by the Model Code only 'reflect the existing state of affairs on Australian campuses'.[55] However, by emphasising the importance of freedom of speech in the university context, and by offering guidance on how free speech could be protected, the Model Code makes a valuable contribution. While there were substantial, if scattered, references to the importance of academic freedom in universities' policies and enterprise agreements prior to the Independent Review, the references to freedom of speech were more sparse. The most contentious debates leading up to the Independent Review were those that focused on attempts to deplatform, disinvite or shut down visiting speakers on campus or to limit the capacity of academics to make publicly express general opinion. The Model Code offers some clarification on these issues.

The Model Code suggests that a broader right to free expression applies when academics wish to make public comments on subjects outside their areas of expertise and that this right should not be constrained due to their being employed by a university. Although the Model Code doesn't require it, universities may wish to encourage academic staff to conduct themselves in accordance with academic norms when exercising this right – that is, by presenting evidence and justification for the views they express and indicating that their views don't reflect those of the university.

On the issue of on-campus freedom of speech, the Model Code recognises two categories of speakers: 'invited visiting speakers', and 'external visiting speakers' who have sought permission to speak on university premises. It accepts that universities may have different requirements for these two categories of speakers, and the code itself would impose stricter requirements on external visiting speakers, in terms of scholarly standards and security costs. This distinction allows universities to support a high degree of free speech for a speaker who has been invited onto campus by a member of the university, but affords it greater power to regulate speakers who merely seek to the use the campus as a venue.

The Model Code also provides that freedom of speech can be constrained where necessary to enable the university to fulfil its duty to foster the wellbeing of staff and students. The question of whether speech can constitute a threat to wellbeing if it has an impact on 'social, cultural, ethnic and religious sensitivities and on vulnerable members of the staff and student communities' is ultimately one that remains unanswered and universities will still have to make difficult decisions about how to balance these responsibilities, a challenge we address in chapter 4 and return to in chapter 6.[56]

Overall, the Model Code positions freedom of speech as a 'paramount value' and academic freedom as a 'defining value'. Little guidance is given as to the relationship between these values, although some provision is made for the idea that the scholarly purposes of a university should condition freedom of speech. For example, a university can refuse to host an external visiting speaker only where their speech purports to be based on scholarship but falls below such standards and would thus do damage to the university's character as a place of higher learning.[57] We will argue in chapter 3 that there is a strong case for a more forthright recognition of the primacy of academic freedom within the context of a university – including within its public square.

Protections Provided in Other Countries

The diversity of mechanisms that characterise the way freedom of speech and academic freedom are protected in Australian universities is seen in other countries too, though the precise regulatory schemes differ. Turning our gaze to Canada, the United Kingdom and the United States, we can see that some universities are provided with official guidance on how to grapple with facilitating free speech while satisfying other duties (the United Kingdom), others are required to adopt policies meeting specified minimum standards (Ontario, Canada and certain states in the United States), and some have the prerogative to determine their own approach to the protection of these freedoms (most states in Canada and the United States).

The United Kingdom

Universities and other higher education institutions in the United Kingdom have a statutory duty to take reasonably practical steps to 'ensure that freedom of speech within the law is secured for members, students and employees of the establishment and for visiting speakers'.[58] The same statute requires the institutional governing body to ensure that the use of its premises is not denied to a speaker on the basis of their beliefs or views, or their policies or objectives.[59] The interaction of this duty with the duties of all public sector bodies to promote equality and to prevent terrorism has been a controversial topic on UK campuses.[60]

In February 2019, the UK Equality and Human Rights Commission published a guide to freedom of expression for higher education providers and student unions in England and Wales. The guide sets out five core principles:[61]

1. Everyone has the right to free speech within the law.
2. Higher education providers should always work to widen debate and challenge, never to narrow it.
3. Any decision about speakers and events should seek to promote and protect the right to freedom of expression.
4. Peaceful protest is a protected form of expression; however, protest should not be allowed to shut down debate or infringe the rights of others.
5. Freedom of expression should not be abused for the purpose of

unchallenged hatred or bigotry. Providers of higher education should always aim to encourage balanced and respectful debate.

The guide also features a flow chart to guide university event planners through the process of identifying, assessing and mitigating obstacles to holding an on-campus event safely and legally.[62] The 'Report of the Independent Review' notes the adaptability of the chart to an events policy for Australian universities that would give 'effect to freedom of expression and academic freedom as paramount values subject to qualifications by law, including duties of care and the duties imposed by the Higher Education Standards'.[63] The guide's flow chart is followed by examples of practical steps event planners can take to mitigate risk and uphold free speech, such as using an independent chairperson to facilitate events; ensuring a range of viewpoints are heard; ticketing events; having a policy in place that sets out principles for respectful discourse; and training staff and students to effectively facilitate debates.[64]

Canada

Free speech controversies have prompted some Canadian universities to adopt comprehensive free speech policies and statements that explicitly delineate the limits of on-campus free speech, especially in cases where upholding it may conflict with other values the university has a duty to protect.[65] The University of Toronto's 'Statement on Freedom of Speech', adopted in 1992, is one example.[66] The statement identifies the university's essential purpose as being 'the pursuit of truth, the advancement of learning and the dissemination of knowledge', a purpose that depends on two conditions: 'an environment of tolerance and mutual respect' and 'as a prerequisite, freedom of speech and expression' for all members of the university. The statement acknowledges that disputes may arise as a result of debate, and urges members of the university to exhibit respect and civility and to 'not weigh lightly the shock, hurt, anger or even the silencing effect' that may be caused by demeaning speech. Ultimately, however, it states that 'the university's primary obligation is to protect the free speech of all involved' and concedes that 'the values of mutual respect and civility may, on occasion, be superseded by the need to protect lawful freedom of speech'. It acknowledges some limits to free speech pertaining to legality, any infringement on the ability of others to exercise free speech, and interference 'with the conduct of authorized university business'.

In August 2018, the Ontario government announced it would require colleges and universities to develop free speech policies meeting minimum standards.[67] The announcement was made in response to recent controversies about free speech and censorship at Canadian universities, including the reprimanding of a teaching assistant at Wilfrid Laurier University for screening a video of psychologist Jordan Peterson defending his refusal to use gender-neutral pronouns. In Ontario, universities are now required to adopt a policy that (1) includes a definition of free speech, (2) states a set of principles based on the Chicago Principles, (3) specifies that existing student discipline measures apply to students whose actions are contrary to the policy (for example, ongoing disruptive protest that interferes significantly with the ability of an event to proceed), (4) states that official student groups' compliance with the policy is a condition for ongoing financial support and institutional recognition, and encourages student unions to adopt policies that align with the university's free speech policy, and (5) provides the possibility to refer free speech complaints that are unresolved through the university's procedures to the state ombudsman.[68] Universities are required to report on their compliance with the policy annually, and they face the threat of funding reductions for noncompliance.

This approach did not find favour in Australia's Independent Review. The 'Report of the Independent Review' describes the Ontario law as 'a rather abrupt and heavy-handed approach', which 'sets an undesirable precedent for executive intrusion into the governance of the sector generally'.[69]

The United States

Academic freedom in the United States has a long history of institutional protection through the American Association of University Professors (AAUP). In 1915, in its 'Declaration on Principles of Academic Freedom and Tenure', the AAUP proclaimed that universities have three purposes: to promote inquiry and advance the sum of human knowledge, to teach students and to develop experts for the public service. It went on to affirm three elements of freedom in universities: freedom of inquiry and research, freedom of teaching, and freedom of extramural utterance and action. The declaration was a response to the threat of interference into academics' areas of research and teaching methods by university administrators and academic boards, and it did not have the support of universities.[70]

The AAUP reached an agreement with the Association of American Colleges twenty-five years later in the '1940 Statement of Principles on Academic Freedom and Tenure'. While affirming the three elements of the freedom identified by the AAUP, the statement added qualifications to each: freedom of inquiry and research was subject to the adequate performance of academics' other duties; academics' freedom of teaching was tempered by the need to be 'careful not to introduce into their teaching controversial matter which has no relation to their subject'; and the freedom of extramural speech was accompanied by 'special obligations' to 'at all times be accurate ... exercise appropriate restraint ... show respect for the opinions of others, and ... make every effort to indicate that they are not speaking for the institution'.[71]

In 2014, in response to a series of incidents in which student protesters attempted to prevent controversial figures from speaking on campus, a Committee on Freedom of Expression was convened at the University of Chicago to draft a statement of the university's commitment to free speech.[72] Its report, a three-page document commonly known as the Chicago Principles (or the Chicago Statement), affirms the view that 'debate or deliberation may not be suppressed because the ideas put forth are thought by some or even by most members of the university community to be offensive, unwise, immoral, or wrong-headed'.[73]

The Chicago Principles represent a strong affirmation of the value of freedom of expression, but provide little practical guidance to universities for preventing and mitigating the conflicts that can arise between free speech and other values. The 'Report of the Independent Review' finds the Chicago Principles to be 'a useful guide to the form of a model code setting out umbrella principles applicable to individual institutions and potentially across the sector – they assert the paramountcy of freedom of expression and the importance of academic freedom, but they also recognise reasonable qualifications'.[74]

Since 2017, a number of US states have passed 'Campus Free Speech Acts – laws that prohibit the creation of designated 'free speech zones' on campuses and require universities to punish students who disrupt speakers on campus. The AAUP is strongly opposed to such legislation, viewing it as unnecessary and likely to have a detrimental effect on the protection of freedoms. As the 'Report of the Independent Review' notes: 'The AAUP concluded that campus free speech laws and academic freedom are "false friends" and that a political agenda is masquerading behind the "free speech" campaign. Model bills were said to exhibit a preference for punishment. It called on faculty members to dispel myths and challenge facile solutions.'[75]

*

Overall, the Independent Review has been valuable for Australian universities. Although it confirmed that nothing approaching a crisis of free speech has occurred in Australian universities, nor any widespread breach of university obligations, the attention to freedom of speech and academic freedom in universities is welcome. One critical matter, in our view, is to recognise that academic freedom and freedom of speech are separate ideas, justified in different ways.[76] Proper responses to the review will depend upon a deep understanding of the underlying concepts. In the next two chapters we explore these central concepts more fully.

3

ACADEMIC FREEDOM

In current and historical debates, the concepts of freedom of speech and academic freedom are much bandied about. They are often used interchangeably or grouped together, as they are in the governing Australian statute, which uses the single and rather nebulous term 'free intellectual inquiry'.[1] There is a reason these two ideas are so prominent. Each is central to the very idea of a university.

Much of the time, running the two ideas together makes little difference, as freedom of speech and academic freedom will often operate in concert to ensure universities are indeed places for free thought and open minds. But we argue there are important distinctions to be made between the two ideas. Freedom of speech is a political freedom that should be enjoyed by all people in democratic nations. Academic freedom has a more specific purpose. It protects the pursuit and dissemination of knowledge through free inquiry and ensures that university research and teaching is authoritative and unbiased.

Understanding this distinction can be important when considering the protection of various types of expression. Expression that exercises free speech rights is justified by general principles applicable to all. Expression that exercises academic freedom is justified by principles more specific to universities. For reasons that we explain in the next two chapters, universities should, in our view, give primary emphasis to academic freedom.

Why Universities Matter

The very etymology of 'university' – derived from *universitas,* the postclassical Latin for a society or corporate body – points to the idea that a university is a *community* of scholars and teachers engaged in a joint intellectual endeavour. That endeavour has a purpose: universities pursue the public good. They advance and disseminate knowledge and in doing so produce tangible benefits for the whole of society.

Advancing Knowledge for the Public Good

Some defenders of universities would prefer to think that the pursuit of knowledge is important for its own sake and does not need to be justified by the identification of any public benefit. In John Henry Newman's nineteenth-century classic *The Idea of a University,* knowledge is valued as it 'own end'. The point of a university education is to cultivate wisdom, judgement and virtue in students, and these qualities should be valued above the achievement of more practical social benefits.[2] Twentieth-century philosopher Michael Oakeshott also objects to the idea that a university's mission or purpose is practical, insisting that intellectual inquiry is simply 'one of the properties, indeed one of the virtues, of a civilized way of living'.[3] This conception of the university has had enduring appeal: pleas are made, to this day, to detach the idea of a university from the practical benefits of its activities.[4]

We sympathise with resistance to the idea that universities are valuable only in so far as they provide specific and tangible benefits. And we agree that research and teaching is too important to reduce to a mere commodity that universities produce in much the same way as other enterprises produce goods and services. Nonetheless, we think it is neither desirable nor realistic to argue, as Oakeshott did, that universities are only important because of their intrinsic value.

To begin with, the argument has not won the day in Australia. The first Australian universities were created to produce suitably qualified professionals to serve the colonies and were modelled on the newer British and Irish universities that showed a greater concern for the practical affairs than may have been true at Oxford and Cambridge.[5] The study of law at the University of Melbourne began in 1857, barely four years after its founding.[6] The University of Sydney provided examinations in law from 1855 and launched a law school in 1890. The lasting practical and utilitarian bent of Australian universities is evident in the way research is funded through the Australia Research Council and National Health and Medical Research Council, which take national research priorities into consideration when determining the distribution of grant funds.

But the point is more fundamental: universities function in relation to the broader society, not in isolation, and the benefits they provide to society are considerable. The benefits of research in science, technology, engineering, mathematics and medicine (the STEMM disciplines) are the most obvious, direct and tangible. Research in these fields – whether basic or applied – has the capacity to help us live longer, healthier lives, create material goods for humans to enjoy, and control and protect our environment. The social sciences (economics, law, anthropology, sociology and political science, for instance) are often highly practical as well, helping us understand and improve our government, economy, social structures and the many other aspects of human society on which they focus. Even disciplines that yield no practical or material benefits of these kinds are enormously important in fundamental ways. Some disciplines – like history and philosophy – help us understand the human consequences of scientific progress and interrogate fundamental ideas such as justice, equality and morality. In short, they can help us understand what a good society or a good life is.

We believe that arguing for universities only in terms of the intrinsic worth of scholarship underestimates their worth and devalues the work they do. Universities benefit the whole of society and if they are to continue to receive public support, it will be dependent on the public understanding that. For these reasons, we argue that the most important and distinctive function of universities is their contribution to the public good by producing and disseminating knowledge through research and teaching.

Do Universities Pursue Knowledge? Can They?

In making this argument for universities, we need to confront some very sceptical ideas about whether universities live up to this ideal. Some critics of universities point to the various ways in which university research can be flawed. But defending the value of academic inquiry as a whole does not require us to defend all academic research. It is, of course, true that academics are flawed. Some may even be incompetent, misguided or dishonest. Problems may come to infect even a whole discipline or subdiscipline. There has been, for instance, a 'replication crisis' in psychology over the past decade. It has become increasingly apparent that researchers are unable to reproduce the results of large numbers of their colleagues' experimental findings, even when those experiments had passed peer review, the process supposedly designed to ensure the integrity of research. Whether the purported crisis reflects real problems within the discipline or can be explained in other ways is beyond our expertise.[7] The point is, however, that problems of this kind, while worthy of serious attention, do not overwhelm the enormous progress in knowledge that universities have produced for centuries.

An even more sceptical idea is that the pursuit of knowledge is not really possible. For most of us, the idea that there are things that we can know, or that something can be true or false, is an uncomplicated idea which we don't often reflect on, but there are some who doubt that there is a 'truth' that academics can reliably discover.[8] 'Truth' is said to be unintelligible or at least inaccessible to humans. Relatedly, it is sometimes argued that the search for truth is so hopelessly infected by the perspectives and biases of the 'truth seeker' that what counts as 'reality' is merely a subjective representation.

There is something ironic about scholars making this kind of claim, as it seeks to undermine the very activity in which they are engaged (and in any event it involves an idea that is itself claimed to be true). If accepted, it could dramatically reshape the case for academic freedom.[9] If there were no possibility of producing knowledge, academic inquiry would be valuable in more limited ways; perhaps it would be as valuable as vocational training, or – as literary theorist Stanley Fish would have it – perhaps it would be 'just a job'.[10] Alternatively, academic inquiry could be recast as a form of political engagement. In any of these scenarios, the case for academic freedom would be drastically narrowed.[11] At best, those academic activities that are expressive (writing, public speaking and the like) would be entitled to a measure of protection under a principle of freedom of speech.

We simply do not share this scepticism about the meaningfulness of academic inquiry. Nor do we think this view is widely shared either inside or outside the academy. Our understanding of the world may be imperfect, but we maintain that some understanding of the world beyond mere subjectivity is possible.[12]

There is another, subtler argument that points to a tension between 'truth' and intellectual inquiry. According to this argument, a belief in a definitive truth might lead some people to justify the suppression of heresy. The famous American jurist Oliver Wendell Holmes, Jr, expresses the idea well in a celebrated dissenting opinion:

> Persecution for the expression of opinions seems to me perfectly logical. If you have no doubt of your premises or your power and want a certain result with all your heart you naturally express your wishes in law and sweep away all opposition.[13]

Tellingly, the idea that universities protect a 'truth' from dissent has resonance with an older understanding of universities as religious institutions designed to impart specific sectarian doctrines or at least to instruct young men in certain received 'wisdom'.[14] Such an idea sits especially uncomfortably with modern understandings of the nature of inquiry in the social sciences and humanities, where the aim is often not to discover facts about the material world but to inquire into morality or politics, or to pursue understanding of literary texts or artistic works. An invocation of 'truth' brings a claim of objectivity and finality to the academic enterprise that academics in these disciplines might regard with unease.

None of these worries undermine the case for university research and the pursuit of knowledge. As we conceive of it, the knowledge that university researchers pursue encompasses moral, religious, ideological and political claims as well as aesthetic and artistic judgements. Knowledge, in this sense, has a human face.[15] It bears the imprint of its maker; it is always somewhat provisional and might well be revised or even overturned. 'Time has upset many fighting faiths,' as Holmes well knew.[16] Especially on moral and political matters, there may never be a final consensus: reasonable disagreement will persist even though we try in good faith to resolve our differences. Where questions are difficult and contested, the discipline of academic study is all the more important.

Academic Methods

Of course, universities are not the only institutions that advance knowledge, but they do so in distinctive ways. Universities pursue knowledge through academic disciplines, which employ methods that are designed to ensure competence and independence in research. Mastering these methods is an important part of the research training that academics undertake. In other words, academics develop *expertise* in the research methods of their disciplines.

The idea of a scientific method is perhaps the best known and most widely understood, but all disciplines have specific methods for subjecting claims to contradiction and interrogation. Among other things, disciplinary methods require researchers to support their theories with evidence and justification, expose them to systematic testing capable of invalidating them and submit them to peer review prior to publication as well as to subsequent criticism and contradiction.

These methods do not make university research infallible. There are instances in which university research has contributed to or directly caused harm. In some cases, the harm was unintended and unexpected, but in others it might be attributed to the flawed moral vision of the researchers. The science of genetics is just one example. It has brought great benefits to humans, but it also made possible the theory and practice of eugenics, which, at least in its most troubling form, was bad science and cruelly racist.[17] The potential for 'academic freedom' to be used as a cover to spread hate and prejudice is an ongoing concern. It is hardly surprising that complex activities like research and scholarship conducted across centuries and continents should have their failures as well as their successes. Most activities can be exploited for good or ill; university research is no exception. The failures vividly illustrate why academic communities have an obligation to impose ethical requirements on their fellow researchers, underlining the importance of both self-examination within disciplines and openness to interdisciplinary insight and external critique.

Academic methods themselves, as well as the results of research, should be challenged. Indeed, for academic methods to remain effective, it is crucial that the very boundaries of a discipline – its system of authority and its priorities – are questioned and open to revision. Our own discipline, law, has been subjected to searing critiques from sociological perspectives, giving rise to sociological jurisprudence, legal realism and critical race and gender theory – frameworks from which many scholars have exposed and criticised flaws in the ideological underpinnings of law and legal scholarship.[18] In legal scholarship, the critical legal studies movement challenged not just the ideological foundations of traditional law, but its traditional methods too. Scholars in this movement were inclined to rely more heavily on narrative and storytelling as a way of bringing 'lived experience' to the understanding of law, and this gave rise to a methodological literature that both criticises and defends this form of scholarship.[19] This kind of critique and revision is part of the academic method itself, and these revisions will, in turn, face their share of analysis. There is no place for mindless authority in any academic discipline.

This rigorous adherence to disciplinary methods (combined with an open-minded willingness to examine, criticise and revise them) makes university research distinctive. While universities cannot claim a monopoly in seeking to advance knowledge and truth, their development and adherence to independently developed research methods give academic research unrivalled breadth, authority and independence. While journalists are also committed to pursuing truth and to writing from a position of independence, they may not have the research expertise that academics do, and they are not part of the broad research mission of universities.[20] Think tanks and commercial research organisations, on the other hand, may aim to advance knowledge across a broad range of research areas, and their researchers may have special expertise; but think tanks may not – and often do not – have the independence of the university academic.

The Case for Academic Freedom

The Pursuit of Knowledge

Armed with the understanding that universities pursue knowledge in distinctive ways, we can now build a positive case for academic freedom. Academic freedom is justified because the advancement of knowledge requires the free inquiry and systematic testing of ideas. In this respect, the argument for academic freedom resembles John Stuart Mill's contention that freedom of speech promotes the search for truth, one of the oldest and best-known arguments for freedom of speech.[21]

Mill's argument relies on the idea that, because humans are fallible, the best way to be assured of truth is to allow all ideas to be freely contested and possibly disproved. Over time and through their constant exposure to contradiction, orthodoxies are revised, bringing ever more assurance (though never complete assurance) of the truth of our understandings.

Mill's proposition that the truth can only emerge through this process of contradiction and re-evaluation has been criticised as being too indifferent to the harms that can be caused by speech and overly optimistic, if not wildly naive, about the capacity of unregulated public discourse to actually arrive at truth. Two faults are commonly identified in relation to public discourse. First, inequality among speakers in terms of their access to the means of communication greatly favours the voices of some – the powerful and wealthy – over others. Second, there is reason to doubt that truth will emerge from discourse if deliberate lying, manipulation and self-interested deception is not regulated.

This critique is much amplified in the digital economy.[22] In modern times, overwhelming amounts of information are easily available to the citizenry at all times, the public's attention span is narrowing, and its capacity to verify information is much degraded by the anonymity of digital communication and the breakdown of confidence in once-trusted sources like legacy media.[23]

These criticisms may be very convincing when Mill's argument is wielded in support of freedom of speech in a general sense. However, they are much less strong when the argument is deployed in support of academic freedom and in the context of academic inquiry. The discipline imposed by academic research methods provides something of an answer to sceptics of Mill's argument. Most speech that causes harm – libel, threats, obscenity, pornography, ordinary racial vilification – could not be justified as part of the academic enterprise. Because of the constraints of academic methods, academic discourse does not resemble a wide-open, unregulated public debate. Indeed, the constraints of the disciplines – the commitment to academic methods, the provision of evidence and justifications – are designed precisely to address the kinds of problems that plague public discourse. These features do not allow academics to claim infallibility – on the contrary, the Millian argument would insist that all claims always be subject to potential invalidation – but they serve as an antidote to the pathologies of an unruly and unregulated 'marketplace of ideas'.

The Argument from Democracy

The core case for academic freedom, as we see it, is that universities pursue knowledge for the public good, and academic freedom safeguards their capacity to do so. But we also want to point to the valuable role academic freedom plays in supporting democratic government.[24]

Once again, there is an affinity between this rationale and arguments for freedom of speech. It is widely accepted that freedom of speech is a necessary condition for democracy.[25] Like Mill's 'argument from truth', the 'argument from democracy' can also be deployed in support of academic freedom if the argument is adjusted to focus on the specific value of independent, systematic and discipline-based research and teaching to democracy.

The argument from democracy can be made for academic freedom in three ways. The first – which is perhaps the more common – claims that a university education produces active, engaged citizens. The idea makes sense.[26] A university education *should* equip students with the knowledge and intellectual skills to support active citizenship. However, we think this argument only offers, at best, a partial justification for academic freedom. After all, not all citizens who are actively engaged in public affairs attended university, and not all university graduates are active citizens: it cannot reasonably be claimed that a university education is either necessary or sufficient for good citizenship.

The second argument is that academic freedom supports democratic governance because universities can provide government with expertise and information. Universities are responsible for training experts who themselves participate in government (judges, high-level administrators, public servants and policymakers of all kinds) or who hold government accountable (journalists and lawyers, among others). University expertise also contributes to a body of knowledge that informs and enables policymaking, providing a foundation for decision-making.

The third argument is perhaps the most persuasive. Academic freedom enables universities to support democracy through the direct provision of information and expertise to the public as a whole. A successful democracy relies on an *informed* citizenry who can actively participate in public discourse, make informed judgements at elections and hold governments to account.[27] The complexity of our current era makes reliable and independent research of the kind that only universities produce more valuable than ever. The coronavirus pandemic of 2020 provides an especially vivid illustration of the point. We need reliable independent information about the public-health crisis so that citizens can hold governments to account for their actions or, indeed, inaction.

Without a proper understanding of the nature of COVID-19 and the threat it poses to us, it is impossible to assess whether governments have responded adequately or whether extraordinary impositions on our freedoms are justified.

But the importance of reliable, unbiased information extends well beyond the health crisis of 2020. We need it to understand myriad public issues, such as the causes and ramifications of climate change, the effect of tax policy on the economy, the morality of assisted dying or even the desirability of banning mobile phones in schools. And we need it to mitigate the impact of information overload, 'fake news' and a breakdown of trust in traditional media. In circumstances of political polarisation, where opposing political forces increasingly present competing versions of the 'facts', the ability to consult reliably independent university research may be one of the few ways to progress political deadlocks.

The importance of free academic inquiry to democracy can be clearly seen in societies where democracy is imperilled. Sadly, authoritarian governments recognise the threat to their power posed by universities: attacks on universities are a standard part of the repertoire of emerging autocrats, as the Hungarian government's campaign to force the Central European University out of Hungary shows.[28] Even in Australia, attacks on universities can sometimes be understood as a political tactic by those who have no desire for their political program to be challenged.

Core Freedoms

Freedom of Research

The scope of academic freedom follows directly from the justifications we have given in the chapter so far. Most obviously, research is protected by academic freedom since, along with teaching, it is central to the pursuit and dissemination of knowledge. However, even this freedom has some limits.

First, academic freedom protects research that plausibly draws on disciplinary expertise and respects disciplinary demands. If academics carelessly disregard the standards of their discipline – if scientists are careless with data, if legal scholars fail to stay on top of changes in the law, if historians misread or fail to consult historical records – academic freedom does not entitle them to immunity from the consequences, which may include being denied university appointments, tenure or promotion. Nor can academics simply abandon their discipline for another discipline or something else entirely. Astronomers cannot rely on the protections of academic freedom to practice astrology, and while we don't wish to take too rigid a view of the boundaries of the disciplines, professors of law cannot claim a freedom to research physics (and vice versa).

For the same reasons, academic freedom does not support a claim to a general freedom of thought unrelated to specialised research. For instance, academics do not, as a matter of course, have the right to access online pornography while at work. If the academics in question were psychologists, political scientists, lawyers or ethicists engaged in researching questions relating to the effect of pornography on the user, the moral status of pornography or the appropriate legal response to pornography, the situation might be considered differently. These academics would be engaged in the pursuit of knowledge – a core activity protected by academic freedom – and were a law or university policy to restrict their access to pornography, it might plausibly be regarded as an infringement of academic freedom.[29] But to make a general claim that academics have the right to access pornography as an aspect of their academic freedom is to misunderstand the concept.

Freedom to Teach and to Learn

Like research, teaching is essential to the advancement of knowledge and academic freedom, and it therefore requires that academics have a degree of autonomy in determining what and how they teach. Decisions about how best to convey ideas and information to students should largely be the purview of academics, either individually or collectively. Whether subject matter is best taught with lectures, discussion-based seminars or practical exercises; what and how much students should read; which method of assessment can be used to evaluate progress most effectively; how to balance discussion, debate and instruction: these are not matters for university administrators to dictate to teaching staff, and still less are they matters for government or another outside regulator to decide.

However, academic freedom has its limits here too. Discipline-specific methods and standards must apply to teaching as much as they do to research, and academic freedom does not give academics an untrammelled right to engage in any behaviour whatsoever during teaching. Academic freedom isn't violated if academics are required to teach material relevant to their course and in accordance with the standards of their discipline. Nor it is an unreasonable limitation to require teaching staff to give some consideration to practical issues, such as financial constraints and classroom availability, which may in turn affect the type of teaching that is possible.

As a corollary of their freedom to teach, academics are obliged to treat students with respect and to teach in a way that engages them. Teachers may challenge students, be demanding and profess strong opinions, but they cannot bully, discriminate or create an environment in which students are effectively unable to express their views. These are not improper limits on academic freedom. They are the classroom equivalents of disciplinary methods and standards: measures that structure and ensure the success of the academic enterprise.

The limits placed on academics in the classroom can be seen as a way of protecting the academic freedom of students. The idea that academic freedom confers some protections on students has a long pedigree. The tradition of academic freedom that was developed in Germany over the course of the nineteenth century explicitly recognises both the academic's freedom to teach (*lehrfreiheit*) and the student's freedom to learn (*lernfreiheit*).[30] The idea was adopted by the AAUP in its influential '1940 Statement of Principles on Academic Freedom and Tenure',[31] and is reflected in the Australian 'Report of the Independent Review', which recognises that all students have a measure of academic freedom.[32]

The freedom to learn should not, however, be mistaken for the idea that students are entitled to determine how and what they learn or how they ought to behave in classrooms or other teaching environments. Such entitlement would, if allowed, come dangerously close to a position (which we reject in chapter 5) that students are the customers or clients of a university's 'business'. Rather, we are arguing that by virtue of the university's mission to advance knowledge, students are entitled to an environment which is properly conducive to learning.

Institutional Freedom

A third element of academic freedom is institutional autonomy. So far, we have focused on the freedom of the individual researcher and teacher. Viewed from this perspective, academic freedom constrains the way a university (through its management) controls the teaching and research work of academics. Subject to the kinds of practical limits on academic freedom that we have already mentioned, university management should not be dictating how and what researchers should study, nor how and what they teach.

But it is also important that universities themselves are free from undue outside influence. Researchers and teachers in universities will not be free to pursue and disseminate knowledge in accordance with their academic judgement if universities are beholden to the political agenda of governments or the interests of wealthy individuals or corporations. On the contrary, there is a risk that research agendas will be driven by the political priorities of the government of the day, or the needs and preferences of the private sector.

It is equally important that Australian universities aren't exposed to the influence of foreign governments as a result of collaborations with overseas universities or as a result of their dependence on the revenue raised by international student enrolment. In chapter 5, we discuss in detail how concerns about university autonomy are growing more pressing as Australian universities become more financially reliant on international students, commercial partnerships and philanthropic donations.

Who Does Academic Freedom Protect?

A final question to consider is who academic freedom protects. It is obvious that academics must be able to exercise academic freedom in relation to teaching and research. And as we have explained, students enjoy a 'freedom to learn'. But what about employees of the university who are not academics? What about laboratory assistants, librarians, research assistants and other individuals who are engaged in research, perhaps as part of a research team or in an assisting or supporting capacity?

This question is often framed in terms of rights: 'Who has the right to academic freedom?' But we resist the idea that academic freedom is a right or entitlement held by an individual. We would reframe the question. Rather than asking who has a 'right' to academic freedom, we would focus on the activity for which protection is claimed. If the activity is part of the research and teaching mission of the university, then that activity and those who engage in it ought to enjoy academic freedom and be subject to its requirements.

The academic freedom that applies to university research will most often be exercised by academics leading research and teaching programs within a university, but the same freedom and limitations should, by our argument, extend to the work of PhD students, research assistants, laboratory assistants and librarians, to the extent, which is often considerable, that they are contributing to scholarship and teaching. A PhD student or laboratory assistant should not be prevented from pursuing research or publishing findings that might offend a donor to the university or upset government officials; a librarian should, likewise, be free from restraints when making information available or assisting with research on topics that might be controversial. In these contexts the scope of academic freedom will reflect the nature of the work – PhD students are properly guided, for instance, by their supervisors, and librarians typically respond to the needs of researchers.

Untangling Freedom of Speech and Academic Freedom

With these fundamental arguments of academic freedom in mind, in the remainder of this chapter we will consider two contexts in which academic freedom and freedom of speech are often confused.

The Classroom Context

Understanding the difference between academic freedom and freedom of speech helps us understand the boundaries of university students' right to speak freely in the classroom. Although we sometimes hear discussions about their right to 'free speech', teaching and learning are activities that are central to the task of advancing knowledge. That's why we suggest that in this context it is much better to understand students as having rights associated with the freedom to learn; it is the value of academic freedom, rather than freedom of speech, that should determine what students can and can't say in the classroom.

In some teaching environments, freewheeling discussion simply won't be part of the activity in which students are engaged. Sometimes teaching requires students to learn specific skills, master specific information or follow technical procedures – think of medical students learning anatomy by dissecting cadavers, or physics or chemistry students conducting experiments in a laboratory. But in many other environments, the presentation and discussion of arguments and opinions are essential for university teaching. In such cases, the academic freedom to learn brings with it a high level of protection for voicing unorthodox, controversial or contrary views.

Nevertheless, some limits will still apply. A university lecturer, for example, may reasonably require classroom contributions to be relevant to the subject under discussion, to be made civilly and to be supported by reason or evidence. Just as academic freedom strongly protects the articulation of unpopular views, it places demands on participants to speak with more rigour and integrity than might be required in a student union debate or a discussion over drinks in the campus bar. When classroom discussion falls below the norms required by the academic setting, teachers have a responsibility to use their judgement and experience to intervene appropriately. They may correct students on a point of inaccuracy or ask them to justify their views or support them with evidence. Some students may interpret such challenges as an affront to free speech, but this shows a misunderstanding of the role of academic freedom in the classroom.

The responsibility teachers have to intervene from time to time in classroom discussion includes an ethical commitment to welcoming and supporting diverse viewpoints. If academics only use their authority to challenge students who do not share their political philosophy or to shut down viewpoints they disagree with, they undermine students' ability to participate, which is an aspect of their academic freedom to learn. The academic freedom that gives teachers a substantial degree of control over what is taught and how it is taught should not become an excuse for excluding students on personal or ideological grounds.

To illustrate this, we could imagine a classroom debate on immigration policy. One student argues vigorously for an open-border policy, saying that it will promote global social justice, antiracism and greater diversity in Australian culture. Another student argues against further immigration, saying that Australia has difficulty absorbing too much cultural diversity, that infrastructure is failing to keep up with population growth and that limiting immigration is the best way to protect the environment. Some members of the class (including the lecturer) may have strong feelings one way or the other on the debate, and some may even be hurt, angered or offended by one of the arguments. Nevertheless, academic freedom protects the right of both students to make their case and neither should face disciplinary action or penalties (such as lower grades) for doing so. If, on the other hand, the student in favour of closed borders were to use a racial slur against his opponent, or if the speaker in favour of open borders were to call her opponent a 'Nazi', then the lecturer would have every right – and even an obligation – to intervene. Academic freedom does not, in our view, protect students if they resort to personal attacks or make assertions with no intellectual value.

When Academics Speak Out

Academics often speak publicly on a wide range of topics – in a professional capacity and as regular citizens. When controversies arise from these comments, the principles of academic freedom and freedom of speech are often invoked interchangeably in their defence. In the light of the distinctions we have already drawn between freedom of speech and academic freedom, it is important to identify when academics are exercising their academic freedom and when they are exercising their right as citizens to engage in freedom of speech. Where academic freedom is involved, we suggest that universities have a very strong obligation to protect the expression of academics and thereby protect the pursuit and dissemination of knowledge. In other cases, rights of free speech apply and while, as we discuss in chapter 4, universities will often want to protect this expression as well, it is not as important to the achievement of the university's central mission.

There are three distinct contexts in which controversies about academic speech arise: when academics discuss research and express expert academic opinion, when academics criticise university governance and when academics offer general public commentary or express non-expert opinion.

Discussing Research and Expressing Academic Opinions

To begin with, academics should obviously enjoy academic freedom when they discuss their research with peers and colleagues and when they discuss matters related to teaching. Such discussions are part and parcel of the pursuit and dissemination of knowledge. Academics might discuss their own ideas and research or the research of other academics. They might also discuss issues related to teaching and assessment and any other matters within their academic expertise.

It is also generally accepted that academic freedom protects academics when they are discussing research or teaching in a public forum. Indeed, in contemporary Australian universities, engagement with the public is regarded as an important and even a required part of academic life. Medical scientists commenting on advances in understanding the causes of Alzheimer's disease, law professors explaining the meaning of court decisions or advocating for legislative change, astrophysicists explaining the nature of the cosmos, historians encouraging the re-examination of past events, an academic from any discipline discussing how best to promote student learning or how teaching and research should interrelate: they are all understood to be exercising their academic freedom, even when engaging publicly with non-experts in their fields.

Because of the importance of the free discussion of research and teaching, an academic may be overtly critical of colleagues, and of their work, in ways that might be out of place in other employment contexts. A frank and vigorous debate between colleagues with different points of view is the epitome of academic freedom in action, and a healthy university environment will support academics who have different views to discuss and who defend their viewpoints in academic literature, the common room and the classroom. Academic discussion also takes place in a public forum, in part because universities encourage public engagement by academics. For this reason, academics should be able to engage in a robust discussion of academic matters even in non-academic environments, including the media. Ideally, such discussion would be respectful, but civility should not be mandated. Passionate advocacy and strong critique can be all too easily mistaken for incivility – especially, perhaps, when the ideas being expressed are challenging and unorthodox. Evidence and reasoning are the touchstones of academic discourse, civility is not.

Unfortunately, this position has not always prevailed in Australian universities. In 2018, Peter Ridd was dismissed from James Cook University for conduct arising out of a dispute about climate-change science. One of the reasons given for his dismissal, which has so far been upheld in the courts, was that he expressed disagreement with colleagues in such a way that it amounted to a breach of his obligation to 'act in a collegial and academic spirit' and treat fellow academics with 'respect and courtesy'. Among the statements for which he was disciplined were comments that his colleagues engaged in 'spin' and would 'wiggle and squirm' when challenged on certain issues.[33] Whatever one thinks of the substance of the scientific dispute itself – and on this we offer no opinion – the requirement for 'civility' or 'collegiality' risks turning a common (if rather unpleasant) form of academic dispute into an occasion for suppressing academic freedom.

On the other hand, if criticism of colleagues or their research veers into bullying or intimidation, it should not be protected. Consider junior academics whose work is repeatedly criticised, denigrated and undermined by a cluster of more senior scholars at their university. In theory, the junior academics have an equal right to respond in kind, and in some environments they may feel free to do so. But the reality is that junior scholars may feel inhibited if they have not yet been confirmed (or tenured) in ongoing positions and are reliant on the support of senior colleagues for career advancement. If senior academics leverage their authority to silence junior staff members, we believe it is a breach of academic freedom because it contributes to an environment that is not conducive to teaching and research. It also breaches the university's duty to protect their employees from bullying in the workplace (part of a more general obligation to obey the law, which we explore further in chapter 4).[34]

Criticising University Governance

At times academics may feel compelled to speak out about their place of work or about universities more generally. Specifically, they may criticise the way their university is governed or may offer critical views of universities in general. It is widely agreed that their right to do so, sometimes called a right of 'intramural expression', is an aspect of academic freedom.[35] This right extends to publicly delivered discussion and criticism, which could include journal articles, lectures or comments made to the media. It does not extend to the defamation of specific individuals, even though universities tend to have, in practice, a relatively high tolerance for defamatory speech.

The logic underlying this freedom is that academics, by virtue of their expertise in research and teaching, are best placed to understand the conditions in which those activities prosper and will be the most motivated to ensure that these activities occur freely and adhere to academic methods.[36] Academic criticism of university governance is therefore essential to the flourishing of research and teaching and, consequently, the pursuit of knowledge.

Early conceptions of the university took the idea that universities should be governed by *academic* standards so seriously that many universities were self-governing institutions. German universities of the nineteenth century were founded on the idea that universities should be collectively governed by academics and that university leadership should not direct academic practices.[37] It was also a feature of the Oxbridge tradition, which influenced Australian universities in spirit, if not in matters of structure and governance.[38]

The form of self-governance seen in Germany and at Oxford and Cambridge has not taken hold in Australia. Australian universities have always been governed not by academics themselves but by an independent governing body appointed by legislators.[39] But this makes academics' freedom to criticise university governance all the more important, for it preserves a place for academic expertise to influence research and teaching. It is a position that lies between the unattainable ideal of full academic self-governance and the dangerous position where academic judgement counts for nought in university governance.[40]

Unfortunately, this aspect of academic freedom is endangered. Many Australian universities have policies or guidelines that allow for action to be taken against staff who undermine the reputation of the university without regard to protecting academic freedom. For example, the University of Melbourne's policy on appropriate workplace behaviour requires employees to 'not intentionally cause serious risk to the reputation or viability of the university, consistent with their employment obligations'.[41] Deakin University's code of conduct requires staff and associates to 'maintain and uphold the reputation of the university, support its goals and act in its best interests'.[42] The University of Western Australia's code of conduct asks employees to consider how their conduct will reflect on the reputation of the university.[43] Flinders University's social media guidelines require staff to consider the impact of posting social media content on the reputation of the university.[44]

Given the importance of academic criticism of university governance, requirements to refrain from criticising your employer – common in other workplaces – cannot be indiscriminately imported into universities. The High Court recently upheld the dismissal of a public servant who was criticising the policies implemented by the department she worked for, even though she did so anonymously over Twitter.[45] An analogous case in a university should be dealt with differently. Consider an academic who believes that university restructuring endangers the proper conduct of research, perhaps by redirecting funding for research into some other matter – or, as in a recent case in Western Australia, an academic who believes that their university does not properly support some of its students, making it difficult for them to succeed academically.[46] Pointing out these matters may well cast the university in a bad light and potentially damage its reputation, but allowing academics to expose these matters is essential to protecting the proper functioning of universities.

The operation of university codes of conduct might be constrained by a contrary provision in an enterprise agreement, but that cannot be assumed. The Federal Court's decision in Peter Ridd's case illustrates the point. Although the James Cook University

Enterprise Agreement obligated the university to protect 'intellectual freedom' and provided that the agreement prevail over inconsistent policies, the court nonetheless upheld Ridd's termination. The court found that 'intellectual freedom' was unclear and could not be equated with academic freedom. In part because of this lack of clarity, the code of conduct – which included requirements for 'collegial' and 'respectful' engagement, and for 'the integrity and good reputation of the university' to be upheld – was found to be consistent with the enterprise agreement.

By contrast, we agree with the Independent Review's finding that it violates academic freedom to impose employment conditions on academics that would prohibit criticising their employer, even though such criticism might at times cast universities in a bad light.[47] Academics need to respect the law and act in accordance with the standards of academic discourse (providing evidence and justification for their views). They also need to respect appropriate standards of confidentiality regarding, for instance, the personal information of students or colleagues. But there will be occasions on which requirements of civility or collegiality will be inappropriate. As Justice Rangiah, the dissenting judge in the Ridd case, pointed out:

> It is difficult to see, for example, how an academic could make a genuine allegation that a colleague has engaged in academic fraud without being uncollegial, disrespectful and discourteous and adversely affecting [the university's] good reputation.

And yet, that kind of accusation may well be essential for research integrity. Equally, where a university departs from governing standards in a way that adversely affects teaching or research, it is important that academics have the freedom to call it out. Academics should not be required to support the university's brand or to avoid embarrassing it if doing so comes at the expense of academic freedom. On the contrary, academics should be able to speak out about research, teaching and university governance even when doing so involves harsh and even disrespectful criticism of their colleagues or university.

A difficult judgement has to be made when academics' criticisms are untrue, malicious or made with reckless indifference to their truthfulness. Some types of criticism made in the public realm can be very damaging to a university's reputation and in extreme cases can have an impact on the financial sustainability of some aspect of its operation. When such commentary is true or at least provided in good faith and with reasonable regard for truth, it should, in our view, be protected. Academics should be given the benefit of the doubt wherever possible, but if an academic does do serious damage through malice, untruthfulness or reckless disregard for the truth, then that conduct falls outside the protection of academic freedom. Academics are the guardians of a culture in which high-quality and independent teaching and research take place. It is impossible for them to carry out that role if they cannot fearlessly call institutions to account, without fear of retribution.

The position we have just outlined leads us to the conclusion that the freedom to criticise the university isn't available to all employees of the university. The freedom to criticise is a measure that allows academics to bring their expertise to bear on university governance, and it is a freedom driven by academic values, not free speech values. Consequently, university staff who are not substantially engaged in research and teaching are not, in our view, protected in the same way.

We do not think, however, that employees have no rights in this sphere. Universities may and arguably should have whistleblower processes that allow any employee with legal or ethical concerns to be heard, usually through confidential channels.[48] There may also be legal recourse if an employee goes public when these channels fail.[49] Furthermore, we believe that universities should strive to have a relatively free and open culture and therefore should have both formal and informal mechanisms to allow all staff – and, indeed, any interested party – to raise concerns about them. But the protection of academics in this regard should be especially strong, given the importance of academic criticism of university governance.

General Public Commentary

The weakest case for academic freedom is a third category of expression sometimes known as 'extramural expression': public commentary that bears no relation to an academic's research or area of expertise. Academics, no less than anyone else, might oppose or support a war, have an opinion on conflict in the Middle East, take a position on same-sex marriage or have strong feelings about any number of social and political issues. And the advent of social media makes this form of commentary all the easier. Should this be within the purview of academic freedom, even where it has no relation to the academic's research expertise?

There is a long American tradition that academic freedom protects all public commentary from academics, reaching back, at least, to the 1915 statement of the AAUP.[50] However, we do not adopt this view, as it appears to rest on the dubious assumption that academics have a special right to engage in general public discourse or a special claim to wisdom on public affairs. The logic of academic freedom, as we understand it, does not support such a claim. In this context it is generally free speech principles that would come into play and potentially serve to protect the academic.

We acknowledge that the distinction between expert commentary and general public commentary may be impossible to maintain in practice. Academic speech may stray from one side of the line to the other in a single communication. That is, an academic might offer both their expert view and their view as a citizen on a single occasion. The widespread use of social media makes this all the more likely. Many academics' Twitter feeds, for instance, contain a mix of personal information, non-expert views on matters of public interest and tweets that are clearly related to their academic expertise. A careful separation of academic and non-academic commentary is simply not possible, and requiring it would likely inhibit academic engagement in public discourse.

A further practical difficulty lies in determining an academic's area of research expertise. Especially in the humanities and social sciences, but potentially in many disciplines, the distinction between research expertise and general opinion is difficult to draw. In the absence of a workable standard, it might be best to allow academics a wide freedom in relation to public discussion (subject to the limits of the law).

Indeed, we should underscore the point that it is in universities' interests to allow all their members broad free speech rights so as to foster a culture of openness that is in turn conducive to research and learning.[51] The reasonable corollary of this position, however, is that academics should exercise a measure of responsibility when speaking in public, conducting themselves in accordance with academic norms of evidence and justification when they are offering a professional opinion and taking care not to identify themselves with the university when they are speaking as regular citizens.

4

FREEDOM OF SPEECH AND ITS LIMITS

Freedom of speech is a universally protected right in the constitutions of the world's democracies and a central tenet of political liberalism.[1] An enormous literature on the justifications for freedom of speech has settled on three principal lines of justification: freedom of speech is essential to the search for 'truth' (the argument from truth), it is necessary for or constitutive of a dignified and autonomous life (the argument from autonomy), and it is a necessary condition for democratic self-government (the argument from democracy).[2]

At the level of political rhetoric, freedom of speech is easy to support. Almost everyone agrees on its importance, and it is often publicly defended, in universities and elsewhere, in rousing terms. Nonetheless, there remain deep and intractable controversies about how freedom of speech is best realised.

For the most part, the debate about freedom of speech in universities focuses on the extent to which otherwise legal speech can or should be restricted. There is a temptation to view any restrictions or burdens placed on public expression as violations of freedom of speech. In public debate, we often hears declarations like 'either free speech is for everyone or no one', 'free speech cannot just be for ideas we like' or the Voltaire-inspired 'I disapprove of what you say, but I will defend to the death your right to say it'.[3] Free speech absolutism is fuelled by many grand statements of principle.

The US Supreme Court is responsible for much of the most inspiring writing about freedom of speech. Justice Benjamin N. Cardozo said, 'Freedom of expression is the matrix, the indispensable condition, of nearly every other form of freedom.'[4] And Justice Robert H. Jackson said, 'If there is any fixed star in our constitutional constellation, it is that no official, high or petty, can prescribe what shall be orthodox in politics, nationalism, religion, or other matters of opinion.'[5]

There is a more than a kernel of truth in these stirring statements. A free speech principle is no principle at all if it gives way at the merest objection. A commitment to free speech is one we have to hold onto even in the face of some unpleasant consequences. However, the reality is that freedom of speech is not truly absolute anywhere, and this has been the case throughout history. In all systems of law and in all serious political thinking, freedom of speech has limits.[6] Freedom of speech is simply too capacious a principle and operates in too many highly complex circumstances for it to be otherwise. Just where those limits lie is a difficult question and answering it requires us to move beyond stirring statements.

The debate about freedom of speech in universities can be confined to a small section of its activities. As we argue in chapter 3, in contexts associated with the universities' teaching and research activities, academic freedom governs the freedom of staff and students to express and debate ideas and share information. Outside of these contexts, there is the scope to discuss a general principle of freedom of speech in universities. Speech that falls under this category usually occurs in the 'public square' of the university rather than its offices, classrooms, laboratories, libraries or residences. This speech can take many forms, including protest and artistic or intellectual expression and debate.

Sometimes it is members of the university community who publicly engage in such activities, other times it is visitors who use the university as a type of public forum. Universities host speakers from outside the academy every day – politicians, public officials, artists, activists and community group representatives among them – and these are largely positive events, compatible with university values and a complement to a lively, intellectual environment on campus.

In many ways, questions about the limits of this speech in universities will be similar to the questions asked about the limits of speech in any other context. Other questions will be more particular to universities and will relate to its specific values. How should universities treat speech that is harmful to other people or detrimental to equality? How should it deal with controversialists and provocateurs who use the university as a platform to cause offence or to insult, deride or speak hatefully about ethnic, religious or sexual minorities? What about flat-earthers, anti-vaxxers and conspiracy theorists who think September 11 was an 'inside job'? This chapter is devoted to the question of how freedom of speech exists in universities and offers some principles that should guide the determination of their limits in the university context.

Freedom of Speech and the Law

Contrary to popular understanding, Australia does not entirely lack constitutional protection for freedom of speech: the High Court has interpreted the Australian Constitution as protecting 'political communication'. The exact boundaries of this concept are still being established, but it is understood to encompass political protest, even unruly protest, and may extend beyond the obviously political to include communication about public affairs more generally. Much of the public speech that occurs on university campuses would therefore be expected to receive some level of constitutional protection, while being subject to reasonable and proportionate limitations.[7]

Other legal protections are found in state and territory law. Victoria, the Australian Capital Territory and Queensland each have charters of rights that require legislators to consider freedom of speech during the lawmaking process.[8] Freedom of speech is also, traditionally, a common-law right that courts pay special attention to in both their rulings and their interpretations of statutes and regulations.[9]

At the same time, Australian law, like all legal systems that protect freedom speech, also regulates speech. Defamation law prevents unjust denigration of reputation, a serious verbal threat may be considered assault, offensive language is prohibited in public spaces, racial and religious vilification may be unlawful, protesters cannot indefinitely obstruct public roads or occupy public spaces, and so forth.

It is important at the outset to realise that universities have no choice but to comply with the general law. An assertion of academic freedom or an elevated right to free speech on campus does not, and cannot, exempt universities from observing the law. Academics, students and university staff have no special freedom to defame, threaten, engage in racial and religious vilification, obstruct public roads or occupy public spaces. Enforcing a law, even a controversial law like section 18C of the *Racial Discrimination Act 1975*, does not indicate that a university lacks respect for freedom of speech.[10] It merely indicates that the university is meeting its legal obligations.

Of course, laws can go too far. In our view, the risk of such overreach is especially high in the realm of national security, where, in the past, governments in Australia and overseas have passed legislation that effectively enlists university staff and resources to suppress or monitor certain types of speech.

A relatively contemporary example is the United Kingdom's counterterrorism laws, which require universities in England, Wales and Scotland to have 'due regard to the need to prevent people from being drawn into terrorism' (known as the 'prevent duty').[11] The Home Office's original guidance on this duty was for universities to disallow events featuring external speakers who were likely to express 'extremist views that risk drawing people into terrorism or are shared by terrorist groups', unless that risk could be 'fully mitigated'. The duty proved controversial, not least of all due to how difficult it was for universities to balance their prevent duties with their obligations to protect freedom of speech and academic freedom.[12] In March 2019, the Court of Appeal found that the guidance government gave universities on this issue was inadequate.[13] The guidance now cites specific obligations for universities, including policies and procedures for managing external speakers and events, carrying out risk assessments and using content filters on IT equipment.[14]

Principles for Limiting Lawful Speech

We can once again return to John Stuart Mill for some first principles. Mill argues that the only justification for limiting liberty of any kind is the prevention of harm against others, an argument that is central to a liberal theory of freedom of expression. What Mill meant by harm is open to interpretation, but there is wide agreement that the prevention of lesser forms of harm do not always sufficiently justify limiting speech. A commitment to freedom of speech must be upheld even in the face of some harms or it is reduced to a mere principle of liberty.[15]

Another way to look at the problem draws on the treatment of free speech in constitutional law. As all democratic constitutions protect freedom of expression, there is a large transnational body of case law addressing its limits in a wide variety of contexts.[16] These cases can help us to structure our thinking on freedom of speech.

Notably, case law tends to focus on two questions. The first is *why* limits to speech are being sought. Or, in other words, what purpose is served by those limits? Restricting protesters from indefinitely obstructing roads reflects the importance of their public use. Defamation laws reflect the worth of personal reputation. Laws against threats and harassment reflect the right to be free of intimidation.[17] It is important to observe that freedom of speech is not the only value our laws protect and at times other values may outweigh it.

Speech might also be limited to ensure that public discussion is reasonably balanced and accurate. In such cases, protection is being sought for the same values – truth, autonomy and democracy – on which free speech itself is premised. Election law provides many examples of this: laws regulate the nature and extent of political advertising and who can donate to political parties and how much. These laws are designed to ensure that all citizens have a relatively equal chance to participate in elections. In Australia, the High Court has, after careful scrutiny, upheld laws targeting corruption and undue influence in the electoral process, even though they may restrict political communication.[18]

The second question case law asks is *how* authorities are seeking to limit speech. Generally, laws restricting free speech should be specific, clear and unbiased. A law that is drawn too broadly will inhibit more speech that can be justified; the law should reflect its purpose. A vaguely drawn law will lead to self-censorship, as speakers will be uncertain what their rights are; the law needs to be reasonably clear. Rules that target speech because of its content or message are usually hard to justify; decisions limiting speech should not reflect the biases of the decision maker. For instance, a law that targets disruptive protest might be harder to justify than a law that targets all forms of disruption. Even more suspect would be a law targeting protests with a certain message (pro-life protesters but not pro-choice protesters, for example).

Harmful Speech and the 'Snowflake' Objection

In debates about freedom of speech in universities, the question of what constitutes harm is one of the most contested. The most obvious kind of harm is physical, but violent threats are typically illegal. The incitement of violence, conspiracy to commit a serious crime and planning for an act of terrorism are all subject to legal sanction, and their prohibition should be uncontentious both in university contexts and beyond, so long as the laws are drafted appropriately.

Harm of a psychological or emotional nature is a more complicated issue. The question of whether to limit speech that causes this type of harm is a debate that has raged for a long time, both inside and outside the academy. It is often discussed in terms of 'hate speech': does hateful speech about a person on the basis of characteristics like race, religion, gender and sexual identity cause harm of a kind that makes restricting speech justifiable?[19]

The question has arisen in some alarming contexts. On American campuses, nooses have been displayed in areas that have a history of lynching, racial slurs have been directed at African-American students and others, and the swastika has been displayed.[20] Australian campuses have their own unhappy history of hate speech, including the use of anti-Semitic and other racist slurs, and the display of Nazi symbols and threatening, anti-Chinese posters demanding that Chinese students 'go home'.[21]

The difficult question for universities is where to draw the line between speech that causes serious emotional harm, thus warranting restriction, and speech that does not. In Australia, the position is somewhat simplified by the law. Many of the most egregious forms of hate speech, such as Holocaust denial and white-supremacist propaganda, are likely be unlawful under the *Racial Discrimination Act.*[22] However, there are always difficult cases at the border of illegality. And some forms of hateful speech – those that target groups defined by their gender or sexual identity, for instance – are often not subject to the law. It is no accident that a number of recent controversies in Australia and elsewhere concern transgender identity and transgender rights.[23]

The traditional liberal position, which favours fewer restrictions on individual freedom, interprets emotionally or psychologically harmful speech as merely causing 'offence' or 'hurt feelings'; even if the offence is extreme, the harm caused is not sufficient to justify restricting speech. From this position, it is often argued that the best way to combat the expression of a hateful idea is to expose and contradict it. As Justice Louis Brandeis put it, 'The fitting remedy for evil counsels is good ones.'[24]

If hurt feelings are all that's at stake, those who object to hateful forms of speech may be characterised as intolerant, intellectually weak and excessively prone to taking offence. The 'snowflake' objection is a modern form of an old charge levelled at supposedly oversensitive students. We do not, however, accept this as a fair characterisation of all objections to hateful forms of speech – in universities or elsewhere.

First, the idea that students are hypersensitive 'snowflakes' is clearly imported from the United States, where politics are more polarised than in Australia and characterised by a distinctive free speech culture not seen in other democracies.[25] The United States' willingness to tolerate highly offensive and damaging forms of expression in the name of free speech is rooted in a deep distrust of government and has produced a highly exceptional body of law. Regulation of even the most hateful forms of speech is generally impermissible, subject to narrow exceptions.[26] By contrast, there is an international consensus that hate speech should be regulated, at least in its more serious forms. There is therefore reason to doubt how well the snowflake objection applies beyond the United States, where the moniker appears to have originated.

Second, it is hard to measure accurately whether a generation is more sensitive or hostile to confronting views than previous generations. As we show in chapter 1, history suggests that students objecting to and shutting down the expression of views they disagree with is no more recent a phenomenon than the suspicion that younger generations are oversensitive and self-indulgent. Some recent studies present evidence that most students today value free speech and believe it is securely protected, even in the United States.[27] A study by King's College London analysed a substantial number of students from across the United Kingdom and shows that a majority of students believe in freedom of speech and are more concerned about its erosion in public life than in their universities. The study also shows that students and members of the general public hold similar opinions on what circumstances justify limiting speech.[28]

Finally, and most importantly, we do not accept that the harm caused by all hateful speech amounts to only hurt feelings or offence. On the contrary, 'snowflakes' may be responding to something real: there is evidence that serious forms of hate speech cause significant emotional harm.[29] Universities must take into account the possibility that their students may be very seriously affected if they are subject to abuse and hate on campus.

Most student counsellors and teachers have witnessed the devastating emotional impact that certain types of speech can have on students and their colleagues. Students and staff can be rude, hostile and disrespectful to each other, and this behaviour can extend beyond the classroom in both the public spaces of a university and in email or social media. In the worst cases, students or staff who are victimised may drop out or resign, fall into depression or even harm themselves. For university leaders, such consequences are not an abstract proposition. Happily, university campuses tend to be much more diverse now than they have been at any other point in our history, but with this diversity comes the challenge of providing a space in which people of different ethnicities, sexualities, religions and cultures can work and study together.[30]

While we agree that speech that merely causes offence or hurt feelings should not be limited in universities, we think it is reasonable for universities to act to protect their communities from the emotional and psychological harms caused by the most serious forms of hateful speech.

*

Another harm associated with some forms of speech is harm to equality. The argument that hateful speech is detrimental to equality was pioneered by the feminist scholar Catherine MacKinnon. The claim contains two broad ideas. First, hateful speech may propagate inequality by conveying the message that members of certain identifiable groups do not have equal standing in society and are not equally deserving of concern, respect and consideration. Second, hateful speech can interfere with the capacity of targeted groups to participate in society and exercise their democratic rights. In particular, it might discourage them from participating in public debate and would thus violate their freedom of speech.

Although this argument began as a radical critique, it has since been adopted by the Supreme Court of Canada, is widely accepted in constitutional law and is influential in courts and academia across the world, even among scholars working squarely within the liberal tradition.[31] In his book *The Harm in Hate Speech,* liberal political philosopher Jeremy Waldron makes a liberal case for the regulation of some forms of hate speech, pointing to a difference between speech that merely causes offence and speech that undermines the dignity and inclusion of vulnerable minorities.[32]

These arguments are especially powerful in university contexts. Equality and the advancement of knowledge are strongly connected.[33] Education and research thrive in an environment of openness where all can participate. An atmosphere of intimidation or contempt is hardly conducive to the pursuit of knowledge and may actually interfere with it. Indeed, it may make it difficult for some people to engage in precisely the kind of intellectual debate that universities wish to promote.

If a group of students and staff are under attack because of their ethnicity, religion or sexuality (and so forth), and the university does nothing to protect them, they may well simply keep to themselves and engage at little as possible in the public and intellectual life of the university. There are always those robust individuals who will be spurred on to make a counterattack, but the response of many others – particularly if they are vulnerable minorities – will be to keep their heads below the parapets in the hope of not becoming a target.

To expand upon this last point, it is worth remembering that all students may be affected by hateful speech, but it is not experienced equally. Women and transgender people will likely bear the brunt of gender-based vilification; ethnic and religious minorities, especially those with a history of discrimination or oppression, are likely to bear the brunt of speech that is racist or anti-religion. In Australia, Indigenous students and scholars, in particular, have been exposed to harmful and denigrating speech in universities. Academic freedom has been used to justify the treatment of the remains of Indigenous people as scientific objects for display and to justify research that purported to demonstrate the intellectual inferiority of Indigenous people.[34] If Indigenous families have concerns about sending their children to university, and if university environments have seemed unwelcoming, it is not surprising. Universities are only now beginning to see substantial Indigenous student enrolments.

Speech without Academic Integrity

A third reason that universities may wish to limit speech arises when the intellectual integrity of the speech is at issue. Some speech starkly contradicts all the best forms of academic evidence, presenting demonstrably false claims – as distinguished from claims that are just controversial or debatable – as true. When such views are expressed within a university, they may also denigrate the integrity or competence of those who work within academic disciplines.[35]

Should universities put up with this? Once again, John Stuart Mill provides a useful starting point for discussion. He argues that the expression of falsity – even patent falsity – should be tolerated, especially where false ideas are articulated and defended by those who believe them. The expression of false ideas can be beneficial because it demands active defence and justification of our true beliefs in response, discouraging complacent and unthinking acceptance of orthodoxy. Buttressing this claim is the argument that governments should not be entrusted with the regulation of speech because they are likely to be incompetent or motivated by corruption or self-interest.

To many, these arguments make a convincing case for tolerating the expression of false claims in the interest of protecting freedom of speech in general society; but, in an age of fake news and climate change denial, tolerating such speech is increasingly controversial.[36] Universities must consider whether allowing such speech conflicts with their responsibility to advance knowledge and uphold scholarly standards.

Individuals from outside of the academy who use universities as a speaking venue may do so to make their arguments seem authoritative or respectable. In other words, they may try to leverage an implied association with a university to convince others that their claims have the same credibility that results from the rigorous evaluation required of academic work. These gambits are a misuse of the university's reputation, and if the public does not understand the difference between an official lecture and public talk given by a fee-paying visiting speaker they have the potential to undermine that reputation. Indeed, universities are regularly criticised for the views expressed by these speakers, as if those views were attributable to the universities themselves.[37]

More fundamentally, universities have a responsibility to advance knowledge in ways that respect the scholarly requirements for evidence and justification, and speakers making false claims do not do so. Mill's argument that the task of dispelling these ideas advances truth is consistent with the principles of academic inquiry. However, when universities host speakers who advance false and even dangerous ideas, it may distract academics and students from the more important work they are engaged in and may even undermine the university's commitment to academic methods of inquiry.

There are good reasons, of course, for universities to be both realistic and cautious when considering whether to deny speakers a platform. We don't suggest that all speakers have to meet the highest standards of academic discourse. In any organisation, there will be plenty of speech that is foolish, ignorant and ill-informed, and universities are no exception. Even if universities strive to do better than the population at large, their members are not immune from being misguided. Rules that tried to ensure all staff, students and visitors adhered to the highest standards of academic rigour would be both overreaching and unenforceable. Further, given the inevitably blurry line between ideas that are unorthodox and truly crazy, the benefit of the doubt should be given to the speaker wherever possible.

Nevertheless, it is important to remember that universities are not mere extensions of the public park or street corner, where anyone can tout their views. On the contrary, universities have a distinctive and important social role, and any claim that they are obligated to provide a platform to all comers, no matter how disreputable their ideas, fails to see how speech can undermine that role, damaging the integrity and reputation of universities.

Facilitating Speech in the Public Square

If it is established that a particular speaker or type of speech is sufficiently harmful or lacking in integrity to justify the university's intervention, it is important to turn to the question of what type of intervention can be justified. Two principles immediately suggest themselves. First, wherever possible, universities should use measures that allow events to go ahead. Second, any restriction on free speech is a restriction on a right and should therefore be as limited as possible and used as a last resort.

In 2007, a controversy blew up at Columbia University when it invited Iranian leader Mahmoud Ahmadinejad to speak at a world leaders forum at the School of International and Public Affairs. A storm ensued: the university was urged to withdraw its invitation and criticised for providing a forum for hate. The event went ahead but Ahmadinejad was introduced by the president of Columbia, Lee Bollinger (himself a noted scholar of free speech).[38] Bollinger pointedly acknowledged the crimes of the Iranian regime, detailing its crackdown on scholars, journalists and human rights advocates, its funding of terrorism and its nuclear program, as well as Ahmadinejad's denial of the Holocaust. He called on Ahmadinejad to answer a series of questions, and more questions from students followed the address, which Ahmadinejad was pressed to answer.

The event was no doubt painful for some members of the Columbia community, especially students and staff who were Jewish, dissenting Iranians or otherwise victims of the regime. But the event was a triumph in another way. It was a profound statement of both Columbia's commitment to freedom of speech and its commitment to reasoned and balanced discussion.[39] Rather than limiting freedom of speech, it facilitated just that kind of public debate to which universities should aspire.

The precise measures that are appropriate will vary from case to case. To assist universities in making the necessary judgements, the UK Equality and Human Rights Commission recommends a number of reasonably practicable steps that universities can take to remove barriers to an event going ahead. These include efforts to promote balanced debate by facilitating opportunities to challenge a speaker's views, using an independent chairperson to ensure a range of views are heard, asking participants to agree to a policy on respectful discourse, and training staff and students on how to conduct a fair debate.[40]

Wherever possible, the university should employ this principle in relation to protests as well. A time-honoured university tradition, student protests have made enormous contributions – for good or ill – to Australian public life. While protesters may on some occasions seek to disrupt the speech of others, protest is itself a fundamental expression of free speech, and any university worthy of the name will respect that right as far as possible, provided protesters are neither violent nor destructive.

It is only as a last resort that universities should restrict controversial speech or speakers. Universities have a legal obligation to protect students and, to some extent, other individuals on campus from injury and other forms of harm. If an event is likely to provoke protests with the potential to give rise to violence or to property damage or other similar kinds of harm, these are grounds for universities to take a directly restrictive approach.[41]

Such an intervention must be governed by a principle of proportionality. The most obvious response to the threat of violent protest is to either prohibit the protest or cancel the event being protested. But these are extreme measures, and the latter in particular risks giving a 'heckler's veto' or effectively censoring certain views.[42] It is a measure that should only be taken in circumstances where all other options have been exhausted and usually where the threat has been externally verified (for example by the police). Wherever possible, a middle path should be trod by such methods as providing security (privately or in partnership with law-enforcement agencies) and restricting how close protesters can come to a venue.

It should be acknowledged that, on some campuses that are especially politically active, the financial cost and disruption associated with facilitating events for controversial speakers have been considerable.[43] To offset the cost, some universities require speakers, protesters or other third parties to pay for the costs of security.[44] Such an arrangement has implications for free speech and may prove practically difficult, particularly if protesters are asked to foot the bill. Protests may be organised with various degrees of formality and be led or attended by people who aren't associated with the university. Additionally, violence and disruption at a protest may be caused by individuals associated with the speaker. Given the importance of balancing the need to protect both public safety and free speech, an expectation that the speaker pay associated security costs may be reasonable, particularly if the speaker comes from outside the university and has sought to use the university as a platform. However, if universities can afford to cover security costs, it will ensure that the speaker's ability to pay isn't a barrier to free speech.[45]

Disciplinary Codes

Universities may seek different strategies to prevent or mitigate harmful speech made by their own staff and students. A common but contentious strategy is the use of codes of conduct and related disciplinary policies to govern student and staff behaviour. Many of the behaviours prohibited by these policies, such as sexual harassment and bullying, are unlawful or highly problematic, and unconducive to a university environment that is respectful, inclusive and safe for all students and staff. However, the policies often go further than this and include requirements that impact on freedom of speech.

The University of New South Wales' code of conduct for its staff, for example, requires that they treat their fellow staff, students and affiliates with 'respect' and communicate with them 'courteously and professionally'.[46] Murdoch University's code of conduct for its students, likewise, requires that they conduct themselves respectfully and, in exercising their freedom of speech, remember their 'responsibility to give consideration to the reputation of the university'.[47] Similar requirements to behave with respect, civility or inclusion are common in many university policies regarding staff and student behaviour.

Although we have no objection to universities using non-punitive approaches to strongly encourage civility, we don't think they should enforce it. There is a difference between behaviour a university might reasonably aspire for its community to exhibit – respect and civility – and behaviour that appropriately leads to disciplinary action. Universities need to tread a careful line between protecting members of the university from harmful behaviour and limiting or inhibiting free speech. As we discuss in chapter 3, if this difference isn't respected, and civility becomes an official requirement for staff and students, it can be misused as a way of silencing troublesome voices or avoiding legitimate criticism. Sigal Ben-Porath captures this danger well in her book *Free Speech on Campus*. As she writes, civility appears to be a reasonable requirement that reconciles the demands of freedom and inclusivity, but it 'leans too strongly to the side of order, reasonableness, and avoidance of challenge.'[48]

To the extent that universities do impose behavioural requirements, the relevant policies should be as clear and as limited in scope as possible – to ensure staff and students don't self-censor permissible speech for fear of falling foul of the provisions – and they should focus on minimising serious and harmful behaviour.

5

EMERGING THREATS: FUNDING MODELS AND RESEARCH PARTNERSHIPS

Universities have undergone a rapid evolution in Australia since the late 1980s, and an especially notable aspect of this evolution is the way funding models have changed. While universities remain heavily reliant on government funding, student fees, industry partnerships and philanthropy are becoming more significant revenue streams as that government funding contracts. In 2018, reliance on international student fees, in particular, had grown to become the biggest source of university revenue (although, due to the coronavirus pandemic, this was no longer the case at the time of writing), and research partnerships with third parties are often viewed as the next important phase for universities.

As Glyn Davis argues, these funding changes have a fundamental impact on the social role of universities:

> When education was free and universities reliant on public funding, they were public institutions in every sense. Now Australia's public universities [have] to raise the majority of their income from students, competitive research grants, philanthropy and commercial activity. Though still public in spirit, and expected to be accountable as public agencies, universities ... rely more heavily on private income.[1]

In other words, the withdrawal of public funding from universities has necessitated the turn to alternate sources of funding, which is not without consequences for the public character of universities.

While an increase in international students, industry partnerships and philanthropic donations are certainly positive developments in many senses, both for universities and the wider community, dependence on these revenue streams carries risks to academic freedom and free speech. The drama of the occasional student protest against a visiting speaker – or heated culture war debates about trigger warnings – diverts public attention from the broader and more complex threats to universities posed by their funding arrangements.

These threats are far less visible and more difficult to assess, and they may also be harder to address – universities may be powerless to control some of the circumstances they arise from, and some threats may need to be accepted as inevitable outcomes of otherwise positive developments. To some minds, particularly those that are hostile to the idea of international and private-sector partnerships (or to partnerships with organisations in particular countries), the answer is to withdraw entirely from such arrangements or subject them to a very high degree of regulation. We believe such a rigid response is unrealistic; we would also view it as another kind of threat to academic freedom, which should allow researchers to collaborate with their partners of choice. There are research questions it may be impossible to pursue without engaging with parties outside the university, and such opportunities should only be denied for very serious reasons, such as the protection of national security.

We therefore think the focus should be on mitigating the inherent risks outlined in this chapter rather than eliminating them. Such an approach requires universities' commitment to academic freedom to be strong enough to withstand commercial, governmental, diplomatic and other forms of pressure.

The Student as Consumer

In Australian universities, students are increasingly expected to foot all or some of the bill for a university education. They are asked to recognise that their education is a private as well as a public good and that they are therefore required to bear their share of the cost. Domestic undergraduate university places are partly subsidised by the federal government and the rest of the cost is covered by student contributions, which may be made through a deferred payment scheme, currently known as the Higher Education Loan Program (HELP). Some postgraduate domestic courses are also subsidised, but others are 'full-fee-paying', meaning students cover the entire cost, potentially with a HELP loan.

In 1986, the government introduced full-fee-paying places for international students (prior to this, international student enrolment was partly subsidised in much the same way as domestic places) and abolished quotas. Together with reduced government funding, this created an ongoing incentive for the sector as a whole to increase the enrolment of international student, as their course fees increase university revenue, subsidise domestic student places and support important research priorities. The number of international students in Australia almost doubled from 366,000 in 2013 to 682,000 in 2019.[2] There have been successful efforts in Australian universities to reach out to the large student markets in countries like China, India and Indonesia, amid increased competition from other countries for those student markets.

The changed funding arrangements were in part an outcome of the extraordinary growth of higher education to a system of mass education. Wholly subsidised tertiary education of a high quality is hard to sustain when a substantial proportion of the population is attending university. The number of Australian university graduates has increased substantially in a relatively short time. In 1966, 160,388 or 1.53 per cent of Australians had a degree.[3] In 2006, the percentage was more than ten times greater, at 17.6 per cent.[4] Ten years later, in 2016 (Australia's most recent census), 2,882,838 or 24 per cent of Australians had a bachelor's degree or higher.[5]

Increased university attendance has had substantial benefits for students, broader society and the economy. It also benefits universities themselves. For most of their history, universities have (either formally or de facto) excluded women, ethnic and religious minorities, and the working class. The growing inclusion of previously excluded or under-represented groups directly increases the diversity of viewpoints expressed in the classroom and in public discourse.

As attendance has grown, the percentage of university fees contributed by students has continued to increase. While both Commonwealth Grant Scheme contributions and student contributions increased between 2004 and 2014, the percentage of student fees increased at a greater rate. Between 2008 and 2018, government funding went from 56.7 per cent of total university revenue to 53.6 per cent, while fees and charges went from 22.2 per cent to 28.5 per cent.[6] International students are typically charged substantially more than domestic students for the same course. In 2020, for example, a Bachelor of Commerce could cost an international student over $120,000 at a leading Australian university or as little as $30,000–40,000 in a lower-ranked university.

One consequence of this trend is that at least some students see themselves as customers of the university, with all the rights and expectations of consumers.[7] While students have historically demanded that universities enact change in the name of justice, equality or a better standard of education, and continue to do so, many contemporary students are making demands of a more commercial nature – they are paying for their education and expect to get their money's worth.

Their expectations encompass both the quality of the university 'experience' and their academic outcomes. Students expect administrative and business processes – enrolment, class registration, applications for special consideration, IT support – to be as efficient as those of the best private providers. That is probably reasonable – there is no virtue in standing in line for hours to be issued a student card and no reason students should have to put up with rude service or poor-quality systems. The expenses of providing this level of quality may, however, divert funding from other important teaching and research priorities.

More troubling for academics, students may also have expectations around the delivery of course content that conflict with the university's idea of high-quality education. Students may pressure universities to 'dumb down' the curriculum, spoonfeed students information or create a teaching experiences that is perceived to be entertaining. The push for online lectures, seminars and tutorials can also reflect a consumerist attitude: 'I am buying this education and I want to be able to access it whenever and wherever is convenient to me.'

More troubling still, students' expectations around academic outcomes may be inconsistent with academic standards. When students expect to pass a class regardless of ability or even honesty, or believe they are entitled to certain grades, pressure is reportedly put on university departments and teachers to ensure paying students are kept happy with the outcome of their studies.[8] Universities must resist this pressure and no doubt most do, but the expectation that fee-paying students will depart the university with the qualification for which they 'paid' is growing.

All this is not to say that universities shouldn't take student concerns seriously. Students are on campus for a relatively short period of time compared to academics and other staff, and their needs can easily be neglected in favour of the interests of longer-term members of the university community. Reasonable expectations about what students will receive from their education should be met. For students to have to settle for whatever teachers are prepared to give and whatever university administrators are prepared to pay for is not satisfactory. Of course, some teachers voluntarily give an exceptional amount in terms of both quality and generosity; such teachers have always existed and continue to today. But for a long time, this dedication was entirely optional and academics could get away with making only a minimal contribution to teaching and student welfare. For those who hark back to the 'good old days', when there was no quality control at all for teaching and no mechanisms for students to express concern or dissatisfaction short of a formal complaint, it should be remembered that some fairly shoddy teaching practices thrived as a result.

Students can also be useful and thoughtful partners in curriculum reform. Their feedback can help universities understand where future areas of interest might be for a course and assess the quality of its teaching. If students are permitted to contribute in this way, it may have other benefits for university learning environments – a different relationship may exist between students and staff, and students may show greater engagement and motivation, and a deeper understanding of the learning process.[9] The ability of students to express their opinions on their university's performance, even if they're not always comfortable for teachers or academic leaders to hear, is an important element of their academic freedom.

Universities are not, however, an educational supermarket, where the customer is always right. Decisions about assessment and grading, course content and delivery are ultimately a matter for informed academic judgement. Academics' decisions on such matters may be usefully informed by the views of their peers, students, industry employers, the pedagogical literature and their own experience. Students may prefer a certain style of course delivery – say, a recorded lecture they can access whenever they want – but, based on their teaching and disciplinary expertise, academics may understand that students' participation in the classroom will lead to better educational outcomes. In law schools, it is traditionally thought that student engagement in debate and discussion is essential to the development of their independent judgement and analytical skills. While acknowledging the benefits of students' feedback and insights, universities must also understand that treating students as consumers has the potential to undermine academic freedom and the educational standards on which students in the end rely.

International Students and the Influence of Foreign Governments

The orientation of Australian universities is becoming increasingly international. International students have become a critical source of revenue for many Australian universities, particularly those with substantial research agendas that can't be supported by current Commonwealth government contributions and domestic student fees. Australian universities are also working collaboratively on a growing number of research projects with universities and other institutions across the globe, seeking to produce research of the highest possible quality. But as beneficial as the internationalisation of the sector continues to be, it also poses challenges to academic freedom and freedom of speech.

The internationalisation of teaching and research in Australia has obvious advantages. As well as funding universities, it substantially benefits the Australian economy (prior to the coronavirus pandemic, higher education was our largest service export); it deepens Australia's connections with other countries and cultures; it gives Australian researchers access to high-quality facilities and research partners in the best universities around the world; it allows universities to recruit first-rate international scholars and to develop enduring relationships with international students who will return home to build their careers (sometimes in positions of influence); and it brings more diversity into the classroom to the benefit of all students. As Monash vice-chancellor Margaret Gardner put it, international students 'form a substantial human bridge' between countries.[10]

A multicultural classroom requires new and thoughtful ways of teaching.[11] Teachers may need to consider ways of structuring classes to help students acclimatise to a different learning culture, especially if students are from countries where learning does not involve classroom participation or where debating issues with an authority figure is culturally inappropriate. If classroom discussion involves criticism of the students' home country, it might be important to ensure other perspectives are articulated. Teachers may also need to take some time, in or out of the classroom, to explain to students why such criticism is allowed in Australia. In many ways, these issues are just particular manifestations of the broader challenge of dealing with controversial speech in the classroom, which can apply equally to Australian students.

One of the benefits of having a diverse student body is that perspectives and experiences are brought into the classroom that might not otherwise exist, and this should be welcomed. If those perspectives include support for governments that are undemocratic, strongly religious or simply different in their political orientations to Australia, this is not a cause for concern in itself. A robust debate on such differences, informed by people who have lived experience, is a wonderful example of the educational possibilities presented by classroom discussion and an important part of students' academic freedom. A more complex challenge arises when it appears that foreign governments or actors are attempting to influence classroom behaviour or course content. This kind of pressure primarily arises in two ways.

The first occurs when a student from another country is offended by class materials or views presented by a teacher, and pressures the teacher to censor or retract those views, potentially through formal or informal government channels. There are only a few examples of this type of behaviour occurring in Australia, and they are somewhat ambiguous.

One incident occurred in May 2017, when a Monash University lecturer used a textbook quiz with a question that mocked the Chinese government and suggested it was dishonest.[12] Chinese students at Monash responded with complaints, and China's consulate-general in Melbourne reportedly questioned the school.[13] The lecturer was temporarily suspended, a decision that Monash emeritus professor J. Bruce Jacobs publicly criticised, and he subsequently left the university voluntarily.[14]

A second incident occurred in August 2017, when a University of Newcastle student confronted a lecturer for referring to a chart that listed Hong Kong, an administrative region of China, and Taiwan, which China claims comes under its jurisdiction, as separate 'countries'.[15] In an interaction that the student filmed, he demanded that the lecturer show more respect for the feelings of the Chinese students in the classroom, while the lecturer said that the student would have to 'learn to accept' hearing different viewpoints.[16] *The Australian* reported that the Chinese consulate-general entered the dispute, but neither the university not the consulate would confirm this, and no action appears to have been taken against the lecturer.[17] According to an article from BBC News, the University of Newcastle 'said it expected staff and students to respect cultural differences and sensitivities' and 'was disappointed that a video had been covertly recorded and leaked'.[18]

A third incident occurred in the same month, when students at the University of Sydney complained that a lecturer had displayed a map showing three regions contested by China and India as Indian territories.[19] The lecturer subsequently issued an apology and said he had mistakenly used an out-of-date map.[20]

Universities are inevitably concerned with protecting international student markets, and they certainly have a responsibility to avoid using incorrect or biased materials in the classroom. But they must also stand firm against any pressure to censor the expression of legitimate views that conflict with the way a foreign nation prefers its history, politics or boundaries to be portrayed. The right of academics to be critical – and critical of powerful interests no less – is a core aspect of their academic freedom. As it appears there are only a handful of incidents like this on the record, it is hard to draw a firm conclusion about whether this is currently a serious issue in Australian universities.

The second way that foreign actors may attempt to influence teaching is perhaps harder for universities to grapple with. This problem arises when international students are self-censoring for fear that other students of the same nationality will report them to their home government if they express certain views, which would result in negative consequences for them or their family.[21] Such pressures clearly impede students' freedom of speech and, by preventing them from participating fully and honestly in classroom discussion, also restrict their academic freedom to learn. For obvious reasons, the extent of the problem is hard to accurately measure and the problem is a very difficult one for universities to address. Students who are self-censoring will rarely report their fears to university authorities, and it may be hard to distinguish them from students who are simply quiet, shy or unengaged. Even if students are willing to share their concerns with a lecturer, it is rare that they will be able to identify an individual who is likely to report on them. And if universities can play a limited role in protecting individual students on campus, there may be little they can do to protect their families at home.[22]

In 2019, Human Rights Watch (HRW) issued guidelines specifically focused on addressing Chinese government interference with academic freedom in other countries.[23] Sophie Richardson, China director at HRW, argues that university's existing mechanisms for protecting academic freedom are out of date:

> Universities can't continue to rely solely on honor codes or other statements of principle designed to address issues like cheating, plagiarism, or tenure to address pressure from the Chinese government on academic freedom abroad ... Those don't envision – let alone set out remedies for – the kinds of threats to academic freedom now widely reported.[24]

HRW recommends that universities develop a statement of academic freedom that encompasses policies on resisting pressure from national and foreign governments and an explicit imperative that classroom discussions must stay on campus and never be reported to foreign governments. It also recommends that universities record instances of foreign government interference, work in concert with other universities to promote international research in China, require the disclosure of foreign government funding granted to student groups, and support scholars if their research is compromised by political interference from foreign governments, by offering them opportunities to change their research strategies or allowing them flexibility with respect to the usual university deadlines.

Although many of HRW's guidelines would be suitable for addressing pressures from other foreign governments, its report's focus is squarely on China. In practice, this selectivity creates some problems for Australian universities. Why, for example, should universities report on funding from China but not from Saudi Arabia or the United States? Why should Chinese student groups be subjected to standards that are not required of student groups from other countries? Apart from the inherent unfairness of taking action against a whole group because of the actions of a few, focusing solely on mitigating Chinese government interference could well foster discrimination against Chinese students and would likely be in breach of anti-discrimination laws in any event. However, if most of these principles were applied regardless of country, they could certainly send a positive and supportive message to international students from a range of countries who might experience pressure from home.

Research Funding and Academic Freedom

In Australia, research is intrinsic to the definition of a university – in fact, to be registered as a higher education provider, an institution must carry out research that 'leads to new knowledge and original creative endeavour'.[25] Funding for research comes from a variety of sources, but the government has long been its primary provider, particularly through competitive grant schemes managed by the Australian Research Council and the National Health and Medical Research Council.

As we discuss in chapter 1, government has at times threatened to make the allocation of this funding contingent on universities toeing the government line, thus infringing institutional autonomy, a key aspect of academic freedom. In more recent years, the personal intervention of Minister Simon Birmingham to disallow grants that had been approved by the Australian Research Council but which he perceived to be in conflict with the public interest has underlined the political danger of universities being wholly reliant on the government for research funding.[26]

While we believe it is reasonable for government to insist that public funds be used for public benefit, to set research priorities in general terms and to channel funds to research projects that have the best chance of success, taking into consideration their design and the researchers and institutions involved, we also believe that academic freedom requires respect for academic expertise in determining which particular projects are to go ahead. Ultimately, decisions about how to spend research funds should be made by academics, not government. In the United Kingdom, this is known as the 'Haldane Principle'.[27]. If governments are too prescriptive about what research is funded, the likelihood of major, fundamental breakthroughs is diminished and academic autonomy is undermined. Academic freedom becomes a myth if researchers are closely managed by governmental directive.

The Australian Research Council and the National Health and Medical Research Council strike this balance by using an expert selection process for individual grants and by requiring grant proposals to identify how research connects to priority research areas, as established by government, and what benefits flow from it. For the most part, Australian governments have respected the compromise struck by this model. But even the occasional intervention is worrying, given the prospect that these interventions may reflect narrow partisan interests and personal or political prejudices.

Different kinds of challenge arise when universities partner with private industries for funding or collaborative purposes. From 2000 to 2016, there was a steady increase in the share of university research income from 'international funding' and 'industry and other funding'.[28] Between 2009 and 2018, it increased from 23.97 per cent to 32.25 per cent.[29]

At their best, private partnerships can produce exciting and innovative research that benefits the economy and promotes human wellbeing. While government funding supports a much wider range of research than would be of interest to the private sector, being too reliant on it puts researchers in a precarious position. Government has its own priorities and agendas – public funding is not necessarily without strings – and even when an independent body administers grants, the politics of the day or an economic crisis (real or politically expedient) can lead to dramatic swings in funding available from the public purse. Having a more diverse group of funding sources provides researchers with some protection from the vagaries of public funding and may enhance the academic freedom of some researchers who want to pursue research that the government would not be prepared to pay for.

Engaging with the world outside the walls of the academy to find solutions to real-world problems can be extremely satisfying for researchers and can open their eyes to new ideas and sources of inspiration. Private partnerships may be directly commercial: the university and a variety of private sector partners might work on developing a drug to cure an illness or on an IT solution to better protect data. Such partnerships have led to important breakthroughs and have the potential to create enduring funding sources that provide ongoing support for university research. Gardasil, the human papillomavirus vaccine, was developed by molecular virologist Dr Jian Zhou and Professor Ian Frazer at the University of Queensland. In order to bring it to market, the university had to work with CSL Ltd, Merck & Co. and

GlaxoSmithKline PLC.[30] According to the university, 'When fully distributed over the next two decades, it is estimated deaths from cervical cancer will be reduced by an estimated 250,000 per annum.'[31] Funding solely from government is rarely going to be sufficient to bring a new vaccine or drug to market; both funding and expertise from private sector companies are generally needed.

Many other university partnerships are uncommercial or not focused on profit. An education faculty, for example, may partner with local schools to work with them on assessing their needs or to test hypotheses regarding the improvement of teaching methods. Medical schools have longstanding relationships with hospitals and health providers that cover training and research alike. Taking such work out of the university and testing it in the wider world can be beneficial both for university researchers and their partners. Ideally, of course, these partnerships also benefit society through improved health or education outcomes, higher employment and new systems or products that meet real needs. Universities are increasingly seeing a role for themselves in tackling 'grand challenges' and 'wicked problems'.[32] By drawing on their expertise in a range of disciplines and partnering with public, private and not-for-profit sector organisations, they can make inroads into some of the most complex challenges facing our society.

While there has been a great deal of focus on the benefits of such partnerships, and the government has strongly promoted them,[33] there are attendant dangers to which universities need to respond. The most obvious is that if private partnerships become the predominant form of university research, research that is fundamental, theoretical, speculative and critical is likely to be marginalised. Applied science, medical research, engineering and technology, and some forms of social science may be heavily rewarded, but at the expense of other forms of science (pure mathematics or theoretical physics, for example) and much of the humanities and social sciences. There are few companies in the private sector that are sufficiently large, wealthy and patient to invest in research without some clear end that is deliverable within a reasonable amount of time.

Physicist Tony Klein notes that the tension between scientific inquiry as a good in its own right and scientific development with clear applied ends has endured for many centuries, with Galileo Galilei arguing for the virtues of the former and Francis Bacon for the latter in the sixteenth century. Klein also argues that the results of basic scientific research (as opposed to applied scientific research) are often discovered to have unexpected uses decades later. Famously, Michael Faraday did not live to see the practical application of his theories about electricity. Similarly, the laser, which was invented in 1960, had little practical application for decades but is now ubiquitous. While it is unlikely that a private company would have supported this research, its ultimate value to society is significant.[34]

Similar observations can be made about research in the humanities and social sciences. Consider those scholars of Chinese language, politics, culture and business who worked in obscurity for many decades while Asia was neglected in the West and then when Japan was assumed to be the future leader of the region. It would have been a very far-sighted business that supported such studies at the time. Yet, over the longer term, as China moves towards being the next global superpower, the work undertaken by these scholars has proved useful to the broader economic interest of many Western countries.

Another concern related to private funding and partnerships is that there is no consensus on how university frameworks for ensuring ethical research can be adapted to deal with the complex ethical questions raised by research partnerships with private entities. The value systems of universities and their researchers can be quite different to those of the private sector, where the focus is on return on investment. For instance, many businesses see knowledge as proprietary and best kept close for commercial advantage. The orientation of universities towards the public good means that their attitude to knowledge has generally been one of openness and sharing, even in relation to institutions that are seen as competitors or that are based overseas. The two cultures may not sit well together, and while sometimes this can be resolved with some goodwill and common sense on both sides, it more often goes unrecognised.

This clash of values may have some troubling consequences when the private-sector partner maintains control over whether and how the results of the research it has funded will be published. For instance, it might bury the results of a drug trial that show a newly developed drug is not as effective as was hoped (or, worse, has serious side effects) and publish another test that shows more positive results. Increasingly, university researchers are pushing back against these constraints, insisting that all results be made available in a timely fashion. They should continue to do so, as such practices are inconsistent with academic freedom and threaten the core mission of university research. Put simply, knowledge is not advanced by research that serves private but not public interests.

A second ethical problem arises in a more subtle way. There is a growing body of evidence suggesting that research outcomes are biased by researchers' self-interest, including their financial interests. Even relatively trivial incentives, such as branded office stationery, have been shown to influence the decisions made by doctors.[35] If a research team can only retain its funding by obtaining the 'right' result, how might that knowledge affect researchers? As universities seek to reward staff for entrepreneurialism by allowing them a financial stake in any commercial outcome, the danger is magnified even further. Researcher bias may be unintentional and unconscious, influencing the judgement of those who have every intention of maintaining the highest standards of ethics and impartiality.

The independence of academic research is one of its defining elements, as is its compliance with an ethical framework. Academic freedom requires that academics be permitted to follow a research question through to its conclusion, even if such a conclusion is uncomfortable for other actors. Universities must support their researchers by ensuring that contracts with private parties uphold these principles and that potentially problematic terms, such as confidentiality clauses, are only used in an ethical matter. It is vital that academic independence is protected by both researchers and by those university leaders who promote industry relationships.

Finally, universities must be alert to the potential for research agendas to focus on the problems and interests of those sectors with available funding, possibly at the expense of research areas that might provide a more significant public benefit. It is sometimes simplistically assumed that if research has tangible social benefits it will attract private-sector funding. If something is worth doing, the logic goes, someone will be willing to pay for it. This is not the case, though of course there are examples of businesses or private philanthropists that do choose to fund research with little regard for a profitable return.[36] If university research has significant public benefits, receiving government support should be a reasonable expectation. While such funding cannot be limitless, its availability allows scholars to tackle important issues that might otherwise be neglected.

Philanthropic Donations

In line with the trend toward external funding, philanthropic donations are a growing source of university revenue. For much of their history, Australian universities were more or less publicly funded; while generous donors made useful contributions, significant reliance on philanthropy was, until recently, rare. In response to this development, universities are finding they must develop practices that allow for productive and ethical relationships with donors.[37]

Donations to universities, especially large donations, are rarely made without clear agreements about how they are to be used. Donors typically want to fund a specific area of research, a teaching program or an aspect of university life for which they have enthusiasm but perceive to be overlooked. A donor may wish, say, to support an area of study by endowing a chair or a research centre for particular purposes, or by providing scholarships for students in certain fields. Such donations, and many others, make major and positive contributions to university life in all spheres. The Minderoo Foundation, for example, is supporting research in areas like clean oceans and Indigenous parity; the Paul Ramsay Foundation funded a research project on how to better support incarcerated parents and their children to break the cycle of intergenerational imprisonment; and the Ian Potter Foundation has long supported projects promoting the arts, social justice, public health and environmental issues.[38]

However, even with the best will in the world, some donors may have expectations that a gift will allow them to influence research and teaching in a manner not compatible with academic freedom. It is not unreasonable for donors to expect some measure of influence, but the more control they seek to assert on the precise direction of teaching and research, the more problematic the relationship can become.

The Ramsay Centre's proposal to donate large amounts to Australian universities to fund the study of 'Western civilisation' brought this issue to the fore. Its vision was quite detailed: students would study 'the great texts of western civilisation (including art and music) in small groups of 6–8, in a sequential arrangement developing an integrated sense of traditions of thought and art going back 2,500 years'.[39] The idea of a private foundation funding a teaching program in this way was novel in Australia. The proposal was also, to some extent, one more battle in a long-running and unproductive culture war.[40] It is perhaps unsurprising, therefore, that controversy ensued. Universities, however, did have legitimate concerns about institutional autonomy. The main issue was the extent to which they would retain control over course content (within the broad area of Western civilisation) and academic appointments. In the end, the agreements reached between the centre and the three universities who will be teaching the degree seem to respect these matters.[41] The University of Queensland's position, that 'the university's autonomy with regard to academic decisions is a red-line issue' and that the university should 'maintain control over staff appointments as well as the curriculum and teaching', seems to us to capture the most important element of institutional autonomy.[42]

Mitigating the Risks of Private-Sector Partnerships

If all of the mechanisms for distributing research funding are in the hands of the private sector, there is a real danger to academic freedom. Government research funding, with peer-reviewed mechanisms for assessing quality, ensures there are funding opportunities available both for research that challenges or is critical of certain private interests and research that is long-term, theoretical or fundamental, or which has no commercial agenda.

Yet government funding is insufficient in itself to mitigate the risks to academic freedom that can be posed by business partnerships. The higher education sector's increasing reliance on private funding requires universities to listen with genuine concern to what their partners need in these partnerships. A relationship that is one-sided, or which is viewed by universities as merely a funding source, is unlikely to be enduring and discourages others in the private sector from partnering with universities. The danger is that universities can go from paying insufficient attention to the needs of industry, as they have been accused of doing in the past, to prioritising those needs above their own legitimate interests and even above academic values.[43] Boundaries still need to be drawn that reflect the distinct ethical demands of university research.

The Australian Code for the Responsible Conduct of Research 2018, which sets out to define 'the broad principles that characterise an honest, ethical and conscientious research culture', grapples with these issues. 'Transparency in declaring interests and reporting research methodology, data and findings' is the third principle it articulates. To fulfil this principle, researchers must 'share and communicate research methodology, data and findings openly, responsibly and accurately' and 'disclose and manage conflicts of interest'.[44] These principles are reiterated in the overview of the specific responsibilities of researchers, which require researchers to 'disseminate research findings responsibly, accurately and broadly' (responsibility 23) and to 'disclose and manage actual, potential or perceived conflicts of interest' (responsibility 24).

A guide developed to support universities with the implementation of the code clarifies that the primary focus of its conflict of interest provisions is personal conflict (benefits to the researcher, their families or their institution, for example) rather than the more indirect influences that may arise from joint research being undertaken with an industry partner.[45] Under the code, the funding arrangements supporting this work would, however, need to be disclosed in any resulting publications. This disclosure would at least alert readers to the potential that research results may have been influenced (perhaps unconsciously) by commercial interests.

In medical research, there has been a shift towards greater transparency, particularly the mandatory disclosure of negative trial results. The main mechanism for compelling this disclosure is the registration of major trials prior to testing and a requirement that the trial results be published on that system. It is certainly an improvement on the previous procedure, which allowed researchers and funding partners to determine what would and wouldn't be disclosed, but there are questions about whether it is as effective as it should be.[46] One of the key benefits of a registration system is that it can eliminate the cherrypicking of favourable results, but this only works if the system is used in an appropriate and timely manner. A 2017 study concludes that 'despite the widespread registration of clinical trials, there remain serious concerns of trial results not being published or being published with a long delay'. It found that, out of seventy-seven studies (backed by $59 million in funding), only 61 per cent published papers within eight years of receiving that funding.[47] Efforts are being made to address these inadequacies, but for now, the system remains fragmented and limited.[48]

In such circumstances, it is important for universities to have a clear sense of their own values and priorities and the courage to pursue them. There are partnerships that are not worth having because they provide too little value to the university. There are others that would require universities to act against their core ethical commitments or central values. The long-term damage that such partnerships can have on universities' reputations are an additional reason for university leaders to refuse them without hesitation.

When universities do enter into partnerships with private-sector entities, they must also insist, in most cases, that research results will be made transparent. This may involve supporting academics against pressure to take on onerous confidentiality clauses. That is not to say that there aren't circumstances in which confidentiality clauses are warranted. The protection of intellectual property, the legal restrictions around classified information, or the privacy of research subjects may well necessitate confidentiality, at least for a period of time. The key is to ensure that confidentiality clauses are justified, ethical and not a de facto control mechanism. In Australia, government research partners are sadly some of the worst offenders when it comes to including and enforcing confidentiality clauses that allow them to control the dissemination of results.[49]

Finally, university leaders may also need to educate private-sector partners about academic values, particularly the importance of free and robust debate to academic freedom. In a typical commercial partnership, a business would not expect to face criticism from its partner or its partner's staff, but academic freedom protects the right of scholars to make such criticisms. If universities decide to enter into research relationships with defence companies, for example, it will almost inevitably lead to loud criticism from students, and often faculty, who believe it is unethical to engage in research of this kind (despite the fact that most universities decline involvement in the development of weapons).[50] Private-sector partners do not always take kindly to this sort of public criticism (and neither does government, for that matter), but, in this situation, academic freedom must be upheld.

Genuine, mutually beneficial partnerships that enhance research and teaching, and benefit the wider community are incredibly valuable. The capacity to create and maintain such relationships will become one of the key hallmarks of successful universities in the future. But as in any business, good decision-making requires the ability to say 'no' as well as 'yes'.

6

FOSTERING OPEN MINDS: SOME PRACTICAL OPTIONS

In this concluding chapter we move beyond general principles to consider more concrete approaches that universities might take to protect academic freedom and freedom of speech. The two most prominent models available to (and often pressed upon) Australian universities are the much-discussed Chicago Principles and the Model Code produced by the Independent Review of Freedom of Speech in Australian Higher Education Providers.

The Chicago Principles have been prominent in recent controversies in the United States. They have been embraced with particular enthusiasm by conservative or libertarian think tanks in Australia, like the Institute for Public Affairs and the Centre for Independent

Studies, which have also been the leading critics of Australian universities.[1] As we will show in this chapter, however, the Chicago Principles are influenced by the highly distinctive context of the First Amendment to the Constitution of the United States of America and are of questionable relevance in Australia.

The Model Code appears to have been conceived of by the proponents of the Independent Review as an opportunity for a similar charter for Australian universities.[2] The result, however, is much better suited to the Australian context and is good starting point for Australian universities.

Our view is that universities need to cultivate a broad and deep culture of openness. Such a culture cannot be created through the adoption of a statement or code developed by others. As the University of Chicago has done, Australian universities need to create their own identities, on their own terms, and cultivate commitment to them within their communities.

The Chicago Principles

In 2014, the president of the University of Chicago appointed a committee to draft a statement addressing the university's commitment to 'free, robust and uninhibited debate and deliberation'. The committee, led by First Amendment scholar Geoffrey Stone, produced a statement of principles, summarising the 'spirit and promise of the university':

> Because the university is committed to free and open inquiry in all matters, it guarantees all members of the university community the broadest possible latitude to speak, write, listen, challenge, and learn. Except insofar as limitations on that freedom are necessary to the functioning of the university, the University of Chicago fully respects and supports the freedom of all members of the university community 'to discuss any problem that presents itself'.[3]

The statement goes on to confirm, in more detail, that the university will not limit speech that individuals finds disagreeable or offensive, despite valuing a 'climate of mutual respect':

Of course, the ideas of different members of the university community will often and quite naturally conflict. But it is not the proper role of the university to attempt to shield individuals from ideas and opinion they find unwelcome, disagreeable or even deeply offensive. Although the university greatly values civility, and although all members of the university community share in the responsibility for maintaining a climate of mutual respect, concerns about civility and mutual respect can never be used as a justification for closing off discussion of ideas, however offensive or disagreeable those ideas may be...

It is for the individual members of the university community, not for the university as an institution, to make those judgments for themselves, and to act on those judgments not by seeking to suppress speech, but by openly and vigorously contesting the ideas that they oppose.[4]

Officially published as the 'Report of the Committee on Freedom of Expression', the statement is commonly referred to as the Chicago Principles. The principles have achieved global prominence, and to some minds they are the gold standard for freedom of speech on campus. At the time of writing, more than seventy universities and college in the United States have adopted them.[5]

Although we can see why the principles have been so influential – they are succinct, beautifully written and inspiring – their relevance to the Australian context is questionable. First, we should be clear that the Chicago Principles, as that name suggests, are general principles only. They do not attempt to distinguish between the various contexts in which speech occurs in universities, nor do they distinguish, as the Independent Review's Model Code does, between the various relationships that speakers have with the university. As we show in chapter 2, the policies in place at different Australian universities have varying legal authority. In some cases, they have the status of law (made pursuant to delegated powers); in other cases, they are enforceable only within the university. Further, all such policies operate in the context of, and must comply with, enterprise agreements. As the Chicago Principles aren't detailed or attentive to context, we don't believe they would function properly in the Australian regulatory scheme or be able to replace the policies that Australian universities currently have in place.

At most, then, the Chicago Principles might be used as a general statement of principles to accompany universities' more carefully constructed, detail-oriented policies. However, we would be concerned if they were uncritically adopted even for this purpose. The Chicago Principles are written firmly within the American tradition of freedom of speech, as protected by the First Amendment, and in them one can hear the echo of Justice Brennan's famous opinion in *New York Times Co. v Sullivan:* 'We consider this case against the background of a profound national commitment to the principle that debate on public issues should be uninhibited, robust and wide-open.'[6] This connection to the First Amendment tradition is part of the strength of the Chicago Principles. As is hinted at in Justice Brennan's reference to a 'profound national commitment', the ideas of the First Amendment are a repository of American identity and First Amendment cases are celebrated for the power of their rhetoric and their capacity to command commitment to a common cause.[7] But the Chicago Principles' close association with a particular national culture may make them less suited to universities in other countries. All democracies protect freedom of speech as a fundamental freedom, but in the United States this freedom is highly distinctive.[8] It is characterised by rules that have little flexibility in their application and by a uniquely high level of tolerance for pornography, racism and other forms of speech that may be considered harmful.[9]

The influence of the First Amendment on the Chicago Principles is especially notable in the narrow definition of exceptions:

The university may restrict expression that violates the law, that falsely defames a specific individual, that constitutes a genuine threat or harassment, that unjustifiably invades substantial privacy or confidentiality interests, or that is otherwise directly incompatibly with the functioning of the university ... But these are narrow exceptions to the general principle of freedom of expression, and it is vitally important that these exceptions never be used in a manner that is inconsistent with the university's commitment to a completely free and open discussion of ideas.

This concern that exceptions will be misused is easily traceable to the strong distrust of government that characterises First Amendment law and which is not evident in other democracies.[10]

The influence of this exceptional understanding of freedom of speech is also notable in what is missing from the Chicago Principles. They contain no mention of equality, diversity or inclusiveness, values that we argue are as important as freedom of speech in enabling universities to fulfil their teaching and research mission. This omission is entirely consistent with First Amendment law, which has long been peculiarly resistant to the introduction of laws designed to provide equal opportunity for participation in public debate or to address other barriers to equality. It is this aspect of First Amendment law that allows independent corporate expenditure in election campaigns to be unlimited and that protects extreme racist speech – like cross burning – from most regulation.[11]

We are not mounting a critique of the First Amendment as it operates within its own sphere (though we note an intense and growing debate in the United States about the insensitivity of First Amendment law to equality concerns).[12] But its central values are not shared by other democracies, all of which protect freedom of speech, but give more room to principles like equality and dignity in determining its limits.[13] In this regard, a useful contrast is provided by the principles articulated by the University of Toronto, which we previously noted in chapter 2. In its 1992 'Statement on Freedom of Speech', the university makes a strong statement about the connection between free academic inquiry and freedom of speech:

> The essential purpose of the university is to engage in the pursuit of truth, the advancement of learning and the dissemination of knowledge. To achieve this purpose, all members of the university must have as a prerequisite freedom of speech and expression, which means the right to examine, question, investigate, speculate, and comment on any issue without reference to prescribed doctrine, as well as the right to criticize the university and society at large.

The statement recognises the importance of debating 'unorthodox ideas, alternative modes of thinking and living, and radical prescriptions for social ills', but also the importance of being able to do so in an inclusive and respectful environment:

> The purpose of the university also depends upon an environment of tolerance and mutual respect. Every member should be able to work, live, teach and learn in a university free from discrimination and harassment.[14]

The values of equity and inclusivity are expanded on in the university's 2006 'Statement on Equity, Diversity and Excellence':

> We believe that excellence flourishes in an environment that embraces the broadest range of people, that helps them to achieve their full potential, that facilitates the free expression of their diverse perspectives through respectful discourse, and in which high standards are maintained for students and staff alike. An equitable and inclusive working and learning environment creates the conditions for our diverse staff and student body to maximize their

creativity and their contributions, thereby supporting excellence in all dimensions of the institution.[15]

The University of Toronto statements provide an alternative way of thinking about freedom of speech in universities. Freedom of speech is highly valued, but if members of the university are not treated as equals and cannot enjoy an environment in which they are able to participate fully, freedom of speech rings hollow. The two universities' statements are not necessarily inconsistent, but they have a difference in emphasis that we think is important.[16] The vision of a university that seriously considers equality as part and parcel of its free speech principles should not be overlooked due to an uncritical reflex to adopt the Chicago Principles.

The Model Code

We turn, now, to the Model Code presented as part of the 'Report of the Independent Review' by Robert French, former chief justice of the High Court. The Model Code is quite a different creature from the Chicago Principles, being much more detailed and designed to be adapted for compatibility with the specific statutory and non-statutory policies that govern Australian universities. It could, as the 'Report of the Independent Review' suggests, operate alongside a non-binding general statement of principles on the model of Toronto or Chicago.[17]

The Model Code is attentive to some matters that are not addressed by the Chicago Principles but which we have argued are important. It recognises, for instance, that academic freedom and freedom of speech are separate concepts, both critically important to universities, and that on-campus speakers may be invited visitors or external visitors, which may affect universities' decisions as to their right to speak on campus.[18]

Rather than recite the Model Code in all its detail, however, we want to focus on its central elements, those being 'The Principles of the Code'. These principles consist of a core statement about freedom of speech – 'Every member of staff and every student enjoys freedom of speech exercised on university land or in connection with the university' – followed by a series of conditions, including:

- 'reasonable and proportionate regulation of conduct necessary to the discharge of the university's teaching and research activities'; and

- 'reasonable and proportionate regulation of conduct necessary to enable to university to fulfil its duty to foster the wellbeing of students and staff.'[19]

By allowing universities to protect their research and teaching mission, these conditions seem to recognise and respect the unique social role that universities play. Elaborating on the first condition, the Model Code specifically provides that the universities may refuse to allow visitors to speak on campus if their speech will or is likely to 'involve the advancement of theories or propositions which purport to be based on scholarship or research but which fall below scholarly standards to such an extent as to be detrimental to the university's character as an institution of higher learning'.[20] Thus the Model

Code does not treat the university as a forum for 'anything goes' political expression, which might characterise the public sphere at large. On the contrary, it recognises that freedom of speech is shaped by the distinct role that universities play in advancing knowledge.

The second of these conditions, which concerns the protection of student and staff wellbeing, implicitly recognises that universities must foster an environment that is conducive to research and learning. Significantly, the Model Code specifically recognises that 'the duty to foster the wellbeing of staff and students' involves a duty to protect staff and students from 'unfair disadvantage or unfair adverse discrimination' and from lawful speech that is 'likely to humiliate or intimidate other persons and which is intended to have either or both of those effects' (we note that the language used here reflects s. 18C of the *Racial Discrimination Act*).

For those who are concerned that these conditions might provide a foothold for spurious limitations on freedom of speech that render the protection worthless, we note that the Model Code also fortifies the commitment to freedom of speech. It specifies that universities cannot deny a platform to an external speaker or invited visitor 'solely on the basis of the content of the proposed speech' and that universities' duty to foster the wellbeing of staff and students 'does not extend to a duty to protect any person from feeling offended or shocked of insulted by the lawful speech of another'.[21]

Our view is that the Model Code represents an acceptable reconciliation of the values of freedom of speech and academic freedom and is a useful starting point for any Australian university wishing to introduce such a code. As we would expect many universities to have a preference for developing their own code or to adapt this one to suit their specific context, we believe adoption of the Model Code should remain voluntary.

A Culture of Openness

Judgements about academic freedom and freedom of speech are implicated in myriad small interactions that occur daily in universities: a teacher conducts a classroom discussion that becomes heated; students assemble to hear a controversial lunchtime speaker; an academic engages with a research partner who wants to limit the release of research results; a discussion in a faculty meeting turns highly critical of university governance; a dean or head of a research centre faces a complaint about a controversial speaker or an outspoken academic. It is neither possible nor desirable for university leadership to be involved in these issues at every point, nor can we realistically expect staff and students to make detailed reference to university policy in the course of day-to-day university life. What universities require is a culture of openness based on a broad understanding of free speech and academic freedom.

How is such a culture to be inculcated? Here we take some

inspiration from the University of Chicago – not from the specific details of the Chicago Principles, but from the way they are given life within the institution. To begin with, the Chicago Principles are a statement of the identity of that university. While its abstract principles are much quoted, it is not often noted that the statement starts by recalling four key historical moments that affirmed the university's commitment to free speech, starting from the early twentieth century and leading up to the present day. Moreover, the principles conclude with the following statement: 'The University of Chicago's long-standing commitment to this principle lies at the very core of our university's greatness. That is our inheritance, and it is our promise to the future.'

Read as a whole, the Chicago Principles are as much about the University of Chicago as they are about freedom of speech. They construct an identity for the university, and this identity is instilled in students throughout their time at the school. Famously, John Ellison, the dean of students at the College of the University of Chicago, wrote to incoming students in 2016 to remind them that a defining characteristics of the university is its 'commitment to freedom of inquiry and expression'.[22] That practice has continued each year.[23] More than the specifics of the letter, which reflect the Chicago Principles, we are impressed by the way the university continuously engages with and reinforces its principles.

The University of Chicago is not the only university to communicate with students in this way. Other college presidents in the United States have also written or spoken to their students on the issue of freedom of speech. In 2018, the president of Princeton University asked students, faculty and staff to read Keith Whittington's *Speak Freely: Why Universities Must Defend Freedom of Speech* over the summer break, in time to discuss it in the first semester.[24]

We have no wish to be prescriptive as to how exactly other universities might foster a culture that respects both academic freedom and free speech.

Universities are best place to decide on matters of tone and emphasis themselves. What is potentially so powerful about these strategies is that they encourage members of a university community to embrace the values of a specific institution in its own context and history. It also recognises that commitments to freedom of expression and academic freedom are not guaranteed. On the contrary, they are values that a university community must collectively imbue in all its members.

Speaking or writing to students and encouraging the university community to educate themselves is only the beginning of this process. We envision that there are many ways, and many forums, in which universities can discuss these matters. We hope that Australian universities will take up this challenge in creative ways that draw on the history and values of their distinct identities. We hope, in doing so, that their subject will be academic freedom as well as freedom of speech. It is a commitment to these values in the hearts and minds of the university community, more than in any specific statement or policy, that would respect the inheritance and fulfil the promise of our universities.

APPENDIX A

A SUMMARY OF THE 'REPORT OF THE INDEPENDENT REVIEW OF FREEDOM OF SPEECH IN AUSTRALIAN HIGHER EDUCATION PROVIDERS'

The 'Report of the Independent Review', written by the Hon. Robert French, was released on 6 April 2019.[1] The Independent Review finds that the claims of a free speech crisis on Australian university campuses are 'not substantiated'.[2] However, within the array of university policies, codes and rules related to free speech and academic freedom, it finds there is too much room for the 'variable exercise of administrative discretions and evaluative judgments', which poses a risk to freedom of speech. This makes the higher education sector 'an easy target for criticism'.[3] Further government regulation is not recommended, primarily because discretion enables institutional autonomy, an important aspect of academic freedom. Rather, clarification of the existing standards is suggested. In this vein, the Independent Review recommends substituting 'freedom of speech and academic freedom' for 'free intellectual inquiry' in the *Higher Education Support Act 2003* and the Higher Education Framework (Threshold Standards) 2015 and adding a definition for 'academic freedom'. Furthermore, the principal recommendation of the report is the adoption by universities, on a voluntary basis, of 'umbrella principles embedded in a code of practice'.[4]

The discussion of the conduct of the review notes that there was no reference to 'academic freedom' in the review's terms of reference. Instead, they referred to 'free intellectual inquiry', the term that appears in the Threshold Standards. French notes the meaning of this term is 'uncertain' but 'seems to cover some elements of academic freedom'.[5] He observes that the term has 'a complex history' and no 'settled definition', but describes it as 'a freedom which, in this context, reflects the distinctive relationship of academic staff and universities' and is regarded as a defining characteristic of universities.[6]

The review identifies institutional autonomy as a key element of academic freedom, referring to 'the capacity of an institution to discharge, in the way it thinks fit, its mission of transmitting and generating human knowledge and conferring on students the skills and abilities which the community is entitled to expect'.[7] It extends to creating and applying rules governing the conduct of staff, students and visitors to the university, and it must be consistent with the discharge of the university's functions, the efficient use of public resources and mechanisms of accountability such as review and parliamentary scrutiny.

The Australian Debate

The review explains it was initiated in response to a perception 'by some in government, and by elements of the community, of a restrictive approach to freedom of speech at Australian universities'. This perception was developed in response to 'a relatively small number of high-profile cases', and the Australian debate was influenced by developments in the United States. The debate centres on questions of how institutions should respond to speech affecting 'social, cultural, ethnic and religious sensitivities' and 'vulnerable members of the staff and student community', what role scholarly standards have in determining who should be allowed to speak on campus, and different views about speech that affects the 'reputation' of the university.[8]

French observes that there is a long history of debate concerning freedom of speech and academic freedom on Australian university campuses, spanning student protests against censorship and obscenity laws and large-scale protests against the Vietnam War and conscription. This history also includes threats posed to academic freedom by inadequate university funding arrangements[9] and ministerial intervention into the allocation of research grants. Recent commentary, however, has focused on internal constraints on free speech and academic freedom, said to come from students and academics themselves. The argument has mainly been advanced by conservative think tanks the Institute for Public Affairs and the Centre for Independent Studies. French notes that contemporary reports of constraints on free speech and academic freedom draw upon the US context and fail to demonstrate a comparable rate of incidents in Australia. Some politicians have also expressed concern recently about free speech on university campuses, departing from earlier commitments to reduce regulatory and compliance burdens upon universities.[10]

The review notes that the higher education sector's responses to the claim of a free speech crisis have varied. In their submissions to the review, university vice-chancellors had expressed different views about the adequacy of the existing regulation of academic freedom and freedom of speech and the need for the Independent Review. For example, French pointed to correspondence from the chief executive of the Go8, which stated that 'Go8 universities already have comprehensive policy frameworks in place'. French cast doubt on this claim, suggesting instead that the number and diversity of university rules on the topic indicates the potential for overreach.[11]

The Independent Review points out that the Australian debate has played out in other countries, and it is valuable to look to these debates, and the responses to them, to inform our response. In this respect, French canvasses the discussion of freedom of speech and academic freedom within universities in the United Kingdom, Canada, New Zealand and the United States.

Response to the Terms of Reference

The review notes that the effectiveness of the *Higher Education Support Act* and the Threshold

Standards to promote and protect freedom of expression and freedom of intellectual inquiry depends upon how they are interpreted by higher education providers and by TEQSA. This is made difficult by the uncertain meaning and scope of 'free intellectual inquiry'. In addition, French observes that these duties must be balanced with others relating to the accommodation of student diversity, the promotion of a safe environment and the fostering of student wellbeing. Currently, policies and practices of universities are diverse and phrased in broad language, and this poses unnecessary risks to freedom of speech and academic freedom.

The review notes that there are a variety of approaches to this issue, as demonstrated by the responses in other countries, ranging from 'legislative prescription to codes of practice to statements of high level principle'.[12] However, French concludes, the 'most realistic and practical options' are the adoption by universities of a statement of principles, operationalised by a code, together with amendments to the *Higher Education Support Act* and the Threshold

Standards which distinguish between academic freedom and freedom of speech and insert a definition of academic freedom.[13] Such an approach is preferable to 'prescriptive legislative requirements' and has the advantage that the sector can claim ownership of it.[14]

Recommendations

Recommendations 1 and 2: Statutory Amendment and Amendment to the Standards

While amendments to the *Higher Education Support Act* and the Threshold Standards are not necessary conditions for universities to adopt a model code, the review states that it is preferable that the terminology in these instruments be clarified. French proposes substituting 'freedom of speech and academic freedom' for 'free intellectual inquiry' in the *Higher Education Support Act* and the Threshold Standards, and introducing a definition of academic freedom.

Recommendation 3: A Model Code

The review proposes a non-statutory model code. The objects of the code are to ensure the freedom of speech of staff, students and visitors to the university is treated as a 'paramount value' and that academic freedom is treated as a 'defining value'. The Model Code presented by the review offers a definition of academic freedom as well as the duty to foster the wellbeing of staff and students. It affirms the freedom of speech and academic freedom of university staff and students, subject only to specified limitations. It states that universities should take steps to minimise restrictions on freedom of speech or academic freedom when entering into arrangements with third parties. In respect of visiting speakers, the Model Code affirms universities may require compliance with booking arrangements and the provision of information, and may refuse permission where a proposed speech is likely to be unlawful or affect the university's duty of fostering wellbeing, or if it purports to be based on scholarship but falls below scholarly standards to such an extent that it is detrimental to the character of the university as a place of higher learning.

APPENDIX B

A CRITICAL REVIEW OF THE INSTITUTE FOR PUBLIC AFFAIRS' 'FREE SPEECH ON CAMPUS AUDIT 2018'

From 2016 to 2018, the Institute for Public Affairs (IPA) produced an annual audit of policies and incidents occurring at Australia's universities related to free speech and academic freedom. These audits draw on similar reports completed by the Foundation for Individual Rights in Education in the United States and Spiked! in the United Kingdom, which rank universities based on their degree of support for freedom of speech. The IPA's audits, written by Matthew Lesh, attempt to measure universities' degree of support for free speech by assessing whether their policies and 'actions' (or incidents) that occur on campus 'limit the diversity of ideas'.[1] They assign university policies and actions one of three colours: red (for policies and actions that are hostile to free speech), amber (for policies and actions that threaten free speech) or green (for policies and actions that promote free speech on campus). They then calculate an overall 'hostility score' for each university by assigning each colour a number and summing up the total score for policies and actions.

The 'Free Speech on Campus Audit 2018' concludes that 'the majority of Australia's universities limit the diversity of ideas on campus' and 'there have been a growing number of censorious actions at Australian universities'. On the basis of the previous two years' audits, the 2018 report also pointed to 'a downward trend in the state of freedom of expression on campus over recent years'.[2]

A number of criticisms can be made of the audits. Key terms are not defined or distinguished; the audits refer to 'free speech', 'freedom of expression' and 'intellectual freedom' without offering definitions of these terms. The methodology is unclear; the ranking of universities is based on the colour assigned to its policies and actions, but the rationale for determining whether a policy or an incident is 'hostile to', 'threatens' or 'promotes' free speech on campus is not explained. Furthermore, when assessing incidents on campus, the author fails to distinguish different actors and their actions. No distinctions are drawn between students who issue an invitation to a speaker, those who protest against the event and the university administrators who respond to the protest. For example, the 2018 audit gives the University of Sydney an amber rating because, in Lesh's words, 'The riot squad was called to the University of Sydney after protesters blocked corridors stopping students who wanted to go to a talk by sex therapist Bettina Arndt.'[3] It is not clear which actor or which action is the subject of the rating. One view is that the university administration's response, in calling the police and shouldering the costs for security, was a positive step for the protection of free speech – an action which 'promoted' free speech – as it allowed Arndt's talk to go ahead.

One of the 2018 audit's key claims is that 'just nine of Australia's 42 universities (21 per cent) have a standalone policy that protects intellectual freedom, as required by the *Higher Education Support Act*'.[4] However, the *Higher Education Support Act* doesn't mandate an explicit policy; it simply states that 'a policy' is required. While Lesh later refers to the purpose of introducing legislation and cites the second reading speech of the Bill introducing this requirement into the Act, he doesn't include the education minister's statement that 'most universities already have such policies and I know they all wish to support research and teaching environments which promote free intellectual inquiry'.[5] In the 2018 audit, unlike in previous audits, Lesh does acknowledge that 'some of Australia's universities do mention academic freedom in either enterprise agreements, or as part of other policies'; however, he goes on to emphasise that these universities 'do not maintain standalone policies on academic freedom'.[6]

The 2017 audit has been convincingly criticised by Professor Glyn Davis for its overreliance on examples from the United States and its failure to provide systematic evidence in support of its key claims.[7] This practice continued in the 2018 audit, which only refers to three incidents in Australia: the dismissal of Peter Ridd from James Cook University, the Australian National University's rejection of the Ramsay Centre and the protests against Bettina Arndt at the University of Sydney. Lesh states that 'these highly publicised incidents, however, are only the tip of the iceberg', suggesting there is 'widespread cultural opposition to free speech'.[8] However, no evidence is provided for this claim; in fact, according to Lesh, such a claim cannot be proven: 'There are ... more incidents not on the public record, and therefore not chronicled in this report because of confidentiality and privacy concerns.'[9] Instead of addressing Davis's criticisms about a lack of evidence, Lesh points to the fact that 'concerns about free intellectual inquiry have been raised by politicians, the human rights commission, commentators from across the spectrum, academics, students, university chancellors, and the higher education union'.[10]

NOTES

INTRODUCTION

[1]   *Ridd v James Cook University* (No.2) [2019] FCCA 2489 (6 September 2019). In a similarly well-publicised incident, Murdoch University removed the associate professor Gerd Schröder-Turk from his university senate position following Schröder-Turk's criticism of the university's admission policies on the ABC program *Four Corners.* In response, Schröder-Turk launched a legal action against the university under whistleblower protection laws, and Murdoch University launched – but dropped after widespread criticism – a counterclaim for damages, arguing that student admissions had declined as a result of Schröder-Turk's comments. Christopher Knaus, 'Academics Condemn "Harassment" of Whistleblower

by Murdoch University', *The Guardian,* 15 October 2019, www.theguardian.com/australia-news/2019/oct/15/academics-condemn-harassment-whistleblower-murdoch-university-schroeder-turk; Dallas Bastian, 'Murdoch University Drops Financial Claim against Whistleblower', *Campus Review,* 15 January 2020.

[2] Arndt would go on to speak at the University of Western Australia on 7 March 2019, despite the UWA and Curtin student guilds calling on the university to cancel her engagement. Elanor Leman, Eliza Huston and Sophie Minissale, 'Bettina Arndt Is Still Set to Speak at UWA Despite Actions from Student Guild and Working Groups', *Pelican Magazine,* 1 March 2019, pelicanmagazine.com.au/2019/03/01/bettina-arndt-is-still-set-to-speak-at-uwa-despite-actions-from-student-guild-and-working-groups.

[3] Gavin Fernando, 'Riot Squad Called to Sydney University Over

Protests to Sex Therapist Bettina Arndt', News.com.au, 12 September 2018, www.news.com.au/lifestyle/real-life/news-life/riot-squad-called-to-sydney-university-over-protests-to-sex-therapist-bettina-arndt/news-story/0698b147e38b44f2b13fc3766664385c.

[4] Bettina Arndt, 'Psychologist Slams Hypocritical Mob of "Abusive" Protesters for Bullying', interview by Chris Smith, *The Chris Smith Show,* 2GB, 24 September 2018, www.2gb.com/psychologist-slams-hypocritical-mob-of-abusive-protesters-for-bullying.

[5] Bettina Arndt, 'Right Wing Commentators Repeatedly Being Slammed with Hefty Bills for Free Speech', interview by Alan Jones, *The Alan Jones Breakfast Show,* 2GB, 11 September 2018, www.2gb.com/right-wing-commentators-repeatedly-being-slammed-with-hefty-bills-for-free-speech. In June 2019, an internal investigation into the incident characterised both the event and

the protest as legitimate manifestations of free speech, finding there was no intent among the protesters to stop the event from occurring. The investigation went on to criticise Arndt for not respecting the investigation's confidentiality and identifying some of the students involved in the protest on social media, leading to the students being subject to derogatory online comments and threats of rape. Michael Koziol, 'Students Given Green Light to Protest after University Dismisses Free Speech Concerns', *The Sydney Morning Herald,* 4 June 2019, www.smh.com.au/politics/federal/students-given-green-light-to-protest-after-university-dismisses-free-speech-concerns-20190604-p51ueo.html.

[6]   Matthew Lesh, 'Free Speech on Campus Audit 2018', Institute for Public Affairs, Melbourne, December 2018, 2.

[7]   Rebecca Urban, 'Universities Declaring War on Free Speech',

The Australian, 10 December 2018; Jeremy Sammut, 'University Freedom Charters: How to Best Protect Free Speech on Australian Campuses', *Policy Paper,* no.10, October 2018.

[8] James Paterson, 'ANU and Western Civilisation Course: Time to Punish Unis That Limit Freedom of Thought', *The Australian,* 18 June 2018, www. theaustralian.com.au/opinion/anu -and-western-civilisation-course-t ime-to-punish-unis-that-limit-free dom-of-thought/news-story/6bfc 31e03935c63b12334121e5256e3 7.

[9] For a critical analysis of the Institute for Public Affairs' work on this question, see appendix B.

[10] Dan Tehan, 'Review into University Freedom of Speech', media release, 14 November 2018, https://ministers.dese.go v.au/tehan/review-university-fre edom-speech.

[11] Robert French, 'Report of the Independent Review of Freedom

of Speech in Australian Higher Education Providers', Department of Education and Training, Canberra, 2019.

[12]   Jay J.V. Bavel, Katherine Baicker, P.S. Boggio et al., 'Using Social and Behavioural Science to Support COVID-19 Pandemic Response', *Nature Human Behaviour,* vol.4, 2020, 460–71; Agnes Callard, 'What Do the Humanities Do in a Crisis?', *The New Yorker,* 11 April 2020; Manuela Gerlof and Rabea Rittgerodt (comps), '13 Perspectives on the Pandemic: Thinking in a State of Exception', De Gruyter, Berlin, www.degruyter.com/staticfiles/craft/media/doc/DG_13perspectives_humanities.pdf.

[13]   'Murdoch University Moves to End Fight with Academic Gerd Schroeder-Turk', *The Australian,* 3 February 2020; *James Cook University v Ridd* [2020] FCAFC 123.

[14]   'Queensland Student Drew Pavlou's Suspension Reduced

but Will Remain Out of University Until 2021', *The Guardian,* 13 July 2020; Michael McKenna, 'UQ Student Drew Pavlou Launches $3.5m Legal Action', *The Australian,* 11 June 2020.

[15] John Ross, 'The World University Rankings 2020: Australia Hits Record High', *Times Higher Education World University Rankings,* 11 September 2019, www.timeshi ghereducation.com/news/world-university-rankings-2020-austra lia-hits-record-high.

CHAPTER 1: HISTORICAL CONFLICTS: STUDENT RADICALS AND PINK PROFESSORS

[1] 'Riotous Day at the University: Communistic Move Resented', *The Age,* 4 May 1932, 9.
[2] 'Riotous Day', 9.
[3] 'Riotous Day', 9.
[4] 'Riotous Day', 9.

[5]   Mathew Lesh, 'Free Speech on Campus Audit 2018', Institute for Public Affairs, Melbourne, December 2018, 2.

[6]   Michael Ignatieff and Stefan Roch (eds), *Academic Freedom: The Global Challenge,* Central European University Press, Budapest and New York, 2018.

[7]   J.M. Main, *Conscription: The Australian Debate 1901–1970,* Cassell Australia Ltd, Melbourne, 1970, 2–3.

[8]   R.M. Crawford, 'Wood, George Arnold (1865–1928)', *Australian Dictionary of Biography,* vol.12, Melbourne University Press, Carlton, Vic., 1990, http://adb.anu.edu.au/biography/wood-george-arnold-9170; Michael Spence, 'Censure and Censorship: Academic Freedom and Public Comment', *The University of Sydney News,* 14 July 2014, http://sydney.edu.au/news/84.html?newsstoryid=13769.

[9]   Robin Archer, Joy Damousi, Murray Goot and Sean Scalmer (eds), *The Conscription Conflict*

and the Great War, Monash University Publishing, Clayton, 2016, 1.

[10]   Phillip Deery, 'Political Activism, Academic Freedom and the Cold War: An American Experience', *Labour History,* vol.98, 2010, 183.

[11]   Jim Allen, 'Childe, Vere Gordon', *Australian Dictionary of Biography,* vol.7, Melbourne University Press, Carlton, Vic., 1979, http://adb.anu.edu.au/biography/childe-vere-gordon-5580.

[12]   Deery, 'Political Activism', 183; Allen, 'Childe, Vere Gordon'.

[13]   Allen, 'Childe, Vere Gordon'.

[14]   Allen, 'Childe, Vere Gordon'; Deery, 'Political Activism', 199, n.1. Phillip Deery notes: 'The only reference in Childe's security files is a comment by Robin Gollan that Childe left Australia because "his left-wing opinions made it difficult for him to get a job here".'

[15]   Deery, 'Political Activism', 183; Allen, 'Childe, Vere Gordon'.

[16] Allen, 'Childe, Vere Gordon'.

[17] Fay Woodhouse, 'Catholic Action and Anti-Communism: The Spanish Civil War Debate at the University of Melbourne, March 1937', *Journal of Australian Studies*, vol, 26, no.72, 2002, 89.

[18] Manning Clark, *The Quest for Grace*, Penguin, Ringwood, Vic., 1990, 44–45.

[19] *Farrago*, 23 March 1937.

[20] M.R. Thwaites, 'Letter to the Editor', *Farrago*, 23 March 1937.

[21] 'Protect Your Freedom: Dr Priestly Condemns Abuses', *Farrago*, 4 May 1937.

[22] 'Protect Your Freedom'.

[23] Diary of Raymond Priestly, 1 December 1936, cited in Fay Anderson, *An Historian's Life: Max Crawford and the Politics of Academic Freedom*, Melbourne University Press, Carlton, Vic., 2005, 66.

[24] See Ellen Schrecker, *No Ivory Tower: McCarthyism and the*

Universities, Oxford University Press, New York, 1986.

[25]   Anderson, *An Historian's Life,* 236.

[26]   John Poynter and Carolyn Rasmussen, *A Place Apart – The University of Melbourne: Decades of Challenge,* Melbourne University Press, Carlton, Vic., 1996, 117.

[27]   *The Sun,* 13 November 1951, cited in Poynter and Rasmussen, *A Place Apart,* 117.

[28]   Poynter and Rasmussen, *A Place Apart,* 118.

[29]   *Gazette,* December 1951, cited in Poynter and Rasmussen, *A Place Apart,* 118; 'University – Forum not Propaganda Machine', *The Age,* 24 December 1951, 3.

[30]   Deery, 'Political Activism', 183, 184. Deery notes that 'methodologically, the lack of evidence of the reasons for the decisions of university selection committees hampers the ability, in some cases, to draw connections between an

applicant's political activity and the decision reached'.

[31] David McKnight, *Australia's Spies and their Secrets*, Allen & Unwin, St Leonards, NSW, 1994, 145.

[32] Anderson, *An Historian's Life*, 236.

[33] Anderson, *An Historian's Life*, 236; McKnight, *Australia's Spies*, 146.

[34] McKnight, *Australia's Spies*, 147.

[35] McKnight, *Australia's Spies*, 145, n.1.

[36] McKnight, *Australia's Spies*, 147.

[37] McKnight, *Australia's Spies*, 148.

[38] Anderson, *An Historian's Life*, 238.

[39] McKnight, *Australia's Spies*, 148.

[40] McKnight, *Australia's Spies*, 148.

[41] Poynter and Carolyn, *A Place Apart*, 117, n.3.

[42] Anderson, *An Historian's Life*, 302.

[43]   Poynter and Rasmussen, *A Place Apart*, 171.

[44]   Poynter and Rasmussen, *A Place Apart*, 187–88.

[45]   Poynter and Rasmussen, *A Place Apart*, 188.

[46]   Poynter and Rasmussen, *A Place Apart*, 117; 'University Should Be a Hotbed', *The Argus*, 5 October 1950; 'Some See University as Communist Hotbed', *The Age*, 5 October 1950; 'University Must Be a Hotbed, Not Refrigerator', *The Sun*, 5 October 1950, cited by Anderson, *An Historian's Life*, 218.

[47]   Sir John Medley, 'University's Good Name: No Propaganda in Our Lecture Rooms', *The Age*, 24 February 1951, 2.

[48]   W.M. O'Neil, 'Anderson, John (1893–1962)' *Australian Dictionary of Biography*, vol.7, Melbourne University Press, Carlton, Vic., 1979, http://adb. anu.edu.au/biography/anderson -john-5017.

[49]   O'Neil, 'Anderson, John'.

[50]   'No Political Freedom: Professor Anderson's Address' *The Sydney Morning Herald,* 11 July 1931, 12.

[51]   O'Neil, 'Anderson, John'.

[52]   'University Professor Censured', *The Brisbane Courier,* 22 July 1931, 19.

[53]   O'Neil, 'Anderson, John'.

[54]   'Reply to University Senate' *The Sydney Morning Herald,* 24 July 1931, 10.

[55]   'Students' Statement', *The Sydney Morning Herald,* 24 July 1931, 10.

[56]   O'Neil, 'Anderson, John'.

[57]   O'Neil, 'Anderson, John'.

[58]   Phillip Deery, 'Scientific Freedom and Post-War Politics: Australia, 1945–55', *Historical Records of Australian Science,* vol.13, no.1, 2000, 1.

[59]   Deery, 'Scientific Freedom', 7; University of New England Selection Committee, 'Confidential File', CSIRO Archives, series 1169, item 16, cited in Deery, 'Scientific Freedom', 7.

[60]   Deery, 'Scientific Freedom', 18.

[61]   Deery, 'Political Activism', 183;
        Anderson, *An Historian's Life*,
        297.

[62]   Anderson, *An Historian's Life*,
        298.

[63]   Frank   Crowley,   'The   Ward
        Fabrication', *Quadrant*, vol.48,
        no.5, May 2004, 30.

[64]   Crowley, 'The Ward Fabrication',
        30.

[65]   Crowley, 'The Ward Fabrication',
        30.

[66]   Hannah Forsyth, 'The Russel
        Ward Case: Academic Freedom
        in Australia during the Cold
        War', *History Australia* vol.11,
        no.3, 2014, 31, 50–51.

[67]   Anderson, *An Historian's Life*,
        298. Anderson later writes:
        'FAUSA ... contacted the
        vice-chancellors to enquire
        whether they practised "political
        discrimination against applicants
        for University positions". They
        responded with a "categorical
        no", but conceded there were
        two exceptions. The first
        involved the ANU, a case that

was apparently resolved, and the second was Ward's case against the University of New South Wales, which was "not satisfactorily clear"' (338).

[68]   Correspondence from Spry to R.G. Menzies, 5 December 1960, NAA: A6119, item 278, folio 97, cited in Deery, 'Political Activism', 183.

[69]   Anderson, *An Historian's Life*, 303.

[70]   Robert Dare, 'Crawford, Raymond Maxwell (Max) 1906–1991', *Australian Dictionary of Biography*, National Centre of Biography and Australian National University, Canberra, 2014, http://adb.anu.edu.au/biography/crawford-raymond-maxwell-max-16260.

[71]   Dare, 'Crawford, Raymond Maxwell'.

[72]   Dare, 'Crawford, Raymond Maxwell'.

[73]   Dare, 'Crawford, Raymond Maxwell'.

[74] Dare, 'Crawford, Raymond Maxwell'.

[75] Anderson, *An Historian's Life*, 178.

[76] Anderson, *An Historian's Life*, 178.

[77] Anderson, *An Historian's Life*, 178.

[78] Anderson, *An Historian's Life*, 179–80. Notwithstanding the damaging allegations levelled against him in April 1961, 'at a time of heightened anxiety about communist infiltration of major institutions', Crawford attracted the ire of his colleagues by writing a letter 'to the *Bulletin* alleging misconduct by an unnamed communist in two unnamed departments at the university. Surprisingly, given his reputation as a civil libertarian sympathetic to reformist causes, he recommended that applicants for academic positions should be examined for their political affiliations.'

[79]   Deery, 'Political Activism', 183, 184.

[80]   Anderson, *An Historian's Life*, 338.

[81]   Anderson, *An Historian's Life*, 338.

[82]   Graham Hastings, *It Can't Happen Here: A Political History of Australian Student Activism*, The Students' Association of Flinders University, Adelaide, 2003, 7; Russell Marks, '"1968" in Australia: The Student Movement and the New Left', in Jon Piccini, Evan Smith and Matthew Worley (eds), *The Far Left in Australia Since 1945*, Routledge, London, 2019, 134.

[83]   'Pamphlet Power', *The Bulletin*, 6 July 1968, 14.

[84]   'Pamphlet Power', 14.

[85]   Evan Smith, Twitter, 4 December 2018, 1.55a.m., https://twitter.com/hatfulofhistory/status/1069892941991170048. Evan Smith commented on the perennial nature of the discourse of universities in crisis, with a photo of a

headline from *The Canberra Times* on 13 May 1970, warning that 'Universities Face a New Dark Age'.

[86] On the origins of deplatforming during this period in the United Kingdom, see Evan Smith, *No Platform: A History of Anti-Fascism, Universities and the Limits of Free Speech,* Routledge, Oxon and New York, 2020.

[87] Barry York, *Student Revolt: La Trobe University 1967 to 1973,* Nicholas Press, Canberra, 1989, 13.

[88] Hastings, *It Can't Happen Here,* 9; *The Age,* 18 August 1969, cited in Hastings, *It Can't Happen Here,* 9.

[89] Hastings, *It Can't Happen Here,* 9. This is interesting given that, in *The Coddling of the American Mind: How Good Intentions and Bad Ideas Are Setting Up a Generation for Failure* (Allen Lane, London, 2018), Greg Lukianoff and Jonathan Haidt blame

overprotective parenting styles and school practices for student activism today.

[90] See John Searle, *The Campus War: A Sympathetic Look at the University in Agony,* Penguin, Harmondsworth, UK, 1972, 145, cited in Hastings, *It Can't Happen Here,* 10.

[91] 'Students in search of a role', *The Bulletin,* 25 May 1968; 'Paris Burns', *The Bulletin,* 18 May 1968, 26.

[92] Marks, '"1968" in Australia', 134.

[93] Marks, '"1968" in Australia', 134.

[94] Rowan Cahill and Terry Irving, 'The Student Mood: Sydney University' *Dissent,* no.23, Spring 1968, 19, 20.

[95] Cahill and Irving, 'The Student Mood', 22.

[96] Cahill and Irving, 'The Student Mood', 22.

[97] Cahill and Irving, 'The Student Mood', 22.

[98] Cahill and Irving, 'The Student Mood', 22.

[99]   'Monash Move on Discipline' *The Age,* 15 May 1968, 11.

[100]   'Vice-Chancellor States His View', *The Age,* 15 May 1968, 1; 'A Call to Action', Reason in Revolt Project, 'Reason in Revolt: Source Documents of Australian Radicalism', 2006, www.reasoninrevolt.net.au/obj ects/images/image_viewer.htm l?d0657,1,1,S.

[101]   Hastings, *It Can't Happen Here,* 20.

[102]   Hastings, *It Can't Happen Here,* 20–21.

[103]   *The Sun,* 1 July 1969, cited in Poynter and Rasmussen, *A Place Apart,* 35–36.

[104]   Piccini, Smith and Worley, *The Far Left in Australia,* 7.

[105]   'Paris Burns', *The Bulletin,* 18 May 1968, 26.

[106]   Judith Brett, *Australian Liberals and the Moral Middle Class,* Cambridge University Press, Melbourne 2003, 141, cited in Marks, '"1968" in Australia', 136.

[107] Evan Smith and John Piccini, 'Old Left, New Left and Australia in the Long 1968', Verso Books, 18 May 2018, www.versobooks.com/blogs/3826-old-left-new-left-and-australia-in-the-long-1968.

[108] Marks, '"1968" in Australia', 135.

[109] Marks, '"1968" in Australia', 135.

[110] Marks, '"1968" in Australia', 138.

[111] Marks, '"1968" in Australia', 140.

[112] Marks, '"1968" in Australia', 140.

[113] Marks, '"1968" in Australia', 141.

[114] Hastings, *It Can't Happen Here*, 18.

[115] Hastings, *It Can't Happen Here*, 18.

[116] Hastings, *It Can't Happen Here*, 18.

[117] Hastings, *It Can't Happen Here*, 19.

[118] Hastings, *It Can't Happen Here*, 34.

[119]   Hastings, *It Can't Happen Here*, 35.

[120]   'Not Guardian of Student Behaviour', *The Advertiser*, 24 April 1969, cited in Hastings, *It Can't Happen Here*, 35.

[121]   Hastings, *It Can't Happen Here*, 35.

[122]   Clive Hamilton, *What Do We Want: The Story of Protest in Australia*, National Library of Australia, Canberra, 2016, 14, 16.

[123]   Cited in Hamilton, *What Do We Want*, 20.

[124]   Hastings, *It Can't Happen Here*, 39.

[125]   Simon Marginson, *Farrago*, 1979, cited in Hastings, *It Can't Happen Here*, 45–46.

[126]   Hastings, *It Can't Happen Here*, 46.

[127]   Hamilton, *What Do We Want*, 28.

[128]   Greg Langley, *A Decade of Dissent: Vietnam and the Conflict on the Australian Home Front,*: Allen & Unwin, North Sydney, 1992, 125.

[129]   Marginson, *Farrago*, cited in Hastings, *It Can't Happen Here*, 45–46.

[130]   Marginson, *Farrago*, cited in Hastings, *It Can't Happen Here*, 45–46.

[131]   'Police Give a Hand in Protest on Sharpeville', *Honi Soit*, 7 April 1960, 1, cited in Hastings, *It Can't Happen Here*, 45–46.

[132]   Marks, '"1968" in Australia', 137.

[133]   Marks, '"1968" in Australia', 137.

[134]   Ann Curthoys, *Freedom Ride: A Freedom Rider Remembers*, Allen & Unwin, Crows Nest, NSW, 2002.

[135]   Tillman Durdin, 'Sydney Students on Freedom Ride to Aid Natives', *The New York Times*, 26 February 1965, cited by Sally Percival Wood, *Dissent: The Student Press in 1960s Australia*, Scribe, Carlton North, 2017, 157.

[136]   Wood, *Dissent*, 158.

[137]   Curthoys, 'The Freedom Ride', 10.

[138]   Evan Smith, '50 Years of Snowflakes', *8AM Playbook,* 4 November 2018, www.researchresearch.com/news/article/?articleId=1378065.

[139]   Smith, '50 Years of Snowflakes'.

[140]   Smith, '50 Years of Snowflakes'.

[141]   Smith, '50 Years of Snowflakes'.

[142]   Smith, '50 Years of Snowflakes'.

[143]   Glyn Davis, 'Special Pleading: Free Speech and Australian Universities', *The Conversation,* 4 December 2018, https://theconversation.com/special-pleading-free-speech-and-australian-universities-108170; French, 'Report of the Independent Review of Freedom of Speech in Australian Higher Education Providers', Department of Education and Training, Canberra, 2019, 13.

CHAPTER 2: LAWS AND REGULATIONS PROTECTING ACADEMIC FREEDOM AND FREEDOM OF SPEECH

[1]   Katharine Gelber, 'The Great Irony in Punishing Universities for "Failing" to Uphold Freedom of Speech', *The Conversation,* h ttps://theconversation.com/the-g reat-irony-in-punishing-universiti es-for-failing-to-uphold-freedom- of-speech-98548.

[2]   'Just nine of Australia's forty-two universities (21 per cent) have a standalone policy that protects intellectual freedom, as required by the *Higher Education Support Act 2003.'* Matthew Lesh, 'Free Speech on Campus Audit 2018', Institute for Public Affairs, Melbourne, December 2018, 2.

[3]   *Higher Education Support Amendment (Demand Driven Funding System and Other Measures) Act 2011* (Cth).

[4]   Explanatory Memorandum, Higher Education Support Amendment (Demand Driven Funding System and Other Measures) Bill 2011, (Cth), 35.

[5]   Commonwealth, *Parliamentary Debates,* House of Representatives, 26 May 2011, 4772 (Peter Garrett).

[6]   Commonwealth, *Parliamentary Debates,* 26 May 2011, 4772 (Peter Garrett).

[7]   *Higher Education Standards Framework (Threshold Standards) 2015* (Cth), s. 6.1(4).

[8]   *Higher Education Standards Framework (Threshold Standards) 2015* (Cth), s. 2.2(1).

[9]   On the connection between students' sense of inclusion within a university environment and their academic success, see Bruce Macfarlane, 'Reframing Student Academic Freedom: A Capability Perspective', *Higher Education,* vol.63, 2012, 719–32.

[10]   Australian Government, 'Guidance Notes', TEQSA,

2017–19, www.teqsa.gov.au/gu idance-notes.

[11]   Australian Government, 'Guidance Notes', 'Diversity and Equity', Guidance Note Version 1.2, 11 October 2017, 2–3.

[12]   Australian Government, 'Guidance Notes', 'Wellbeing and Safety', Guidance Note Version 1.2, 8 January 2018, 1.

[13]   French, 'Report of the Independent Review', 196–97.

[14]   French, 'Report of the Independent Review', 18.

[15]   Commonwealth, *Parliamentary Debates,* 26 May 2011, 4772 (Peter Garrett).

[16]   Commonwealth, *Education, Employment and Legislation Committee Estimates,* Senate, 25 October 2018, 174–45, cited in French, 'Report of the Independent Review', 35.

[17]   French, 'Report of the Independent Review', 14.

[18]   *Ridd v James Cook University* [2019] FCCA 997 (16 April 2019) para. [94].

[19] *Education Act 1989* (NZ) s. 161(2).

[20] *Education Act 1989* (NZ) s. 162(4)(a)(v); see also D. Gareth Jones, Kerry Galvin and David Woodhouse, 'Universities as Critic and Conscience of Society: The Role of Academic Freedom', AAU Series on Quality No 6, New Zealand Universities Academic Audit Unit, March 2000.

[21] See Terence Karran, 'Free Reign? The Question of Academic Freedom', *Wonkhe,* 9 January 2017, https://wonkhe. com/blogs/free-rein-the-questio n-of-academic-freedom.

[22] *Education Reform Act 1988* (UK) s. 202(2)(a).

[23] Universities UK, 'Freedom of Speech on Campus: Rights and Responsibilities in UK Universities', Universities UK, 2011, www.universitiesuk.ac.uk /policy-and-analysis/reports/Do cuments/2011/freedom-of-spee ch-on-campus.pdf.

[24]   Universities UK, 'Freedom of Speech on Campus', 9.

[25]   *University of Melbourne Act 2009* (Vic.) s. 5(e)(iii).

[26]   *University of Melbourne Act 2009* (Vic.) ss 12(3)(b) and 13(2)(b).

[27]   *Central Queensland University Enterprise Agreement 2017* [2018] FWCA 1445 (9 March 2018), cl. 43.1.

[28]   *Central Queensland University Enterprise Agreement 2017* [2018] FWCA 1445 (9 March 2018), cl. 43.3.

[29]   University of Melbourne, Academic Freedom of Expression Policy (at 30 May 2018), [4.5].

[30]   RMIT University, 'Academic Freedom and Responsibility', accessed 10 December 2020, www.rmit.eu/content/rmit-ui/en/about/our-values.

[31]   RMIT, 'Intellectual Freedom Policy', RMIT Policy Register, accessed 10 December 2020, https://policies.rmit.edu.au.

[32]   University of Western Australia, 'A Code of Ethics and a Code of Conduct', January 2014, 12.

[33]   University of Western Australia, 'University Charter of Student Rights and Responsibilities', 30 October 2000, [4.1(g)].

[34]   Bond University, 'Media Policy', 18 February 2019, [2.3].

[35]   Flinders University, 'Responsible Conduct of Research Policy', 29 June 2016, [3].

[36]   Charles Darwin University, 'Code of Conduct', 15 December 2017.

[37]   University of Southern Queensland, 'Student Code of Conduct Policy', 15 June 2017.

[38]   University of Melbourne, 'Student Conduct Policy', 30 August 2019.

[39]   Monash University, 'Ethics Statement Policy', 29 January 2018.

[40]   Curtin University, 'Research Management Policy', January 2019.

[41]   University of Canberra, 'Charter of Conduct and Values', 11 December 2015.

[42]   Dan Tehan, 'Review into University Freedom of Speech', media release, 14 November 2018, https://ministers.dese.gov.au/tehan/review-university-freedom-speech.

[43]   Tehan, 'Review into University Freedom of Speech'.

[44]   Tehan, 'Review into University Freedom of Speech'.

[45]   French, 'Report of the Independent Review', 13.

[46]   French, 'Report of the Independent Review', 217.

[47]   French, 'Report of the Independent Review', 217.

[48]   French, 'Report of the Independent Review', 20.

[49]   French, 'Report of the Independent Review', 14.

[50]   French, 'Report of the Independent Review', 14.

[51]   French, 'Report of the Independent Review', 14.

[52]   French, 'Report of the Independent Review', 223.

[53]   Deborah Terry, 'Universities Shine in the Contest of Ideas', *The Australian,* 19 June 2019, www.theaustralian.com.au/com mentary/universities-shine-in-th e-contest-of-ideas/news-story/1 fc91a4519df2b3e695d83b758b0 f8bc.

[54]   The University of Sydney is one of the universities that has chosen to modify its existing policies. The Australian Catholic University and Griffith University are among those that have adopted the Model Code in an amended form.

[55]   Katharine Gelber and Kristine Bowman, 'Dan Tehan Wants a "Model Code" on Free Speech at Universities – What Is It and Do Unis Need It?', *The Conversation,* 23 June 2019, h ttps://theconversation.com/dan -tehan-wants-a-model-code-on- free-speech-at-universities-wha t-is-it-and-do-unis-need-it-1191 63. Gelber and Bowman go on to add that 'although universities, their staff and

students all stand to benefit from clarifying obscure policy language, the pressure for universities to take action may be more about politics than anything else'.

[56]   French, 'Report of the Independent Review', 20.

[57]   Principle 6(d) of the 'Model Code for the Protection of Freedom of Speech and Academic Freedom in Australian Higher Education Providers', in French, 'Report of the Independent Review', 235.

[58]   *Education (No 2) Act 1986* (UK) Section 43(1).

[59]   *Education (No 2) Act 1986* (UK) Section 43(2).

[60]   Section 149 of the *Equality Act 2010* establishes the public sector equality duty, which requires all public authorities to have regard to the need to eliminate discrimination, harassment and victimisation and to advance equality of opportunity and foster good relations between people who

share a relevant 'protected characteristic' (age, disability, gender assignment, pregnancy and maternity, race, religion or belief, sex, sexual orientation) and those who do not. Section 26 of the *Counter-Terrorism and Security Act 2015* establishes the prevent duty, which requires specified authorities to 'have due regard to the need to prevent people from being drawn into terrorism'. Under this legislation, universities must also have particular regard to the duty to ensure freedom of speech and the importance of academic freedom: Section 31(2) of the *Counter-Terrorism and Security Act 2015*.

[61] Equality and Human Rights Commission, *Freedom of Expression: A Guide for Higher Education Providers and Students Unions in England and Wales*, Equality and Human Rights Commission, London, February 2019, 6.

[62] Equality and Human Rights Commission, *Freedom of Expression,* 32.

[63] French, 'Report of the Independent Review', 64.

[64] Equality and Human Rights Commission, *Freedom of Expression,* 43.

[65] Peter MacKinnon, *University Commons Divided: Exploring Debate and Dissent on Campus,* University of Toronto Press, Toronto, 2018.

[66] University of Toronto Governing Council, 'Statement on Freedom of Speech', University of Toronto, 28 May 1992, https://governingcouncil.utoronto.ca/secretariat/policies/freedom-speech-statement-protection-may-28-1992.

[67] Office of the Premier, 'Upholding Free Speech on Ontario's University and College Campuses', media release, 30 April 2018, https://news.ontario.ca/en/backgrounder/49950/upholding-free-speech-on-ontarios

-university-and-college-campuses.

[68]   Office of the Premier, 'Upholding Free Speech'.

[69]   French, 'Report of the Independent Review', 79.

[70]   Eric Barendt, *Academic Freedom and the Law: A Comparative Study,* Hart Publishing, Oxford, 2010, 161, 168.

[71]   American Association of University Professors and Association of American Colleges, '1940 Statement of Principles on Academic Freedom and Tenure', AAUP, www.aaup.org/file/1940%20Statement.pdf.

[72]   For more detailed analysis of the *Chicago Principles* see chapter 6.

[73]   Committee on Freedom of Expression at the University of Chicago, 'Report of the Committee on Freedom of Expression', University of Chicago, 2014, https://provost.uchicago.edu/sites/default/files/documents/reports/FOECommitteeReport.pdf.

[74] French, 'Report of the Independent Review', 99.

[75] French, 'Report of the Independent Review', 91.

[76] French, 'Report of the Independent Review', 14.

CHAPTER 3: ACADEMIC FREEDOM

[1] *Higher Education Support Act 2003* (Cth) s 19.115.

[2] John Henry Newman, 'Knowledge as Its Own End', in Frank M Turner (ed.), *The Idea of a University,* Yale University Press, New Haven, Ct, 1996, 79.

[3] Michael Oakeshott, 'The Idea of a University', in Timothy Fuller (ed.) *The Voice of Liberal Learning: Michael Oakeshott on Education,* Yale University Press, New Haven, Ct, 1989, 96.

[4] Raimond Gaita, 'To Civilise the City', *Meanjin,* vol.71, no.1, 2012, 64.

[5] Glyn Davis, *The Australian Idea of a University,* Melbourne

University Press, Carlton, Vic., 2017, 34–38.

[6] John Waugh, *First Principles: The Melbourne Law School 1857–2007*, Miegunyah Press, Carlton, Vic., 2007.

[7] Scott E. Maxwell, Michael Y. Lau and George S. Howard, 'Is Psychology Suffering From a Replication Crisis?' American Psychologist, vol.70, 2015, 487.

[8] For one such account, grounded in philosophical pragmatism, see Stanley Fish, *Versions of Academic Freedom: From Professionalism to Revolution*, University of Chicago Press, Chicago, 2014, 24–28.

[9] David M. Rabban, 'Can Academic Freedom Survive Postmodernism?' *California Law Review*, vol.86, no.6, 1998, 1377; Thomas L. Haskell, 'Justifying the Rights of Academic Freedom in the Era of "Power/Knowledge"', in Louis Menand (ed.), *The Future of Academic Freedom*, University of

Chicago Press, Chicago, 1995, 43.

[10]   Fish, *Versions of Academic Freedom.*

[11]   We have sympathy for the view that without the production of knowledge, there is little point to the academic enterprise and very little case for academic freedom. Larry Alexander, 'Academic Freedom', *University of Colorado Law Review,* vol.77, no.4, 2006, 883, 896; but see Fish, *Versions of Academic Freedom,* 25.

[12]   Rabban, 'Can Academic Freedom Survive Postmodernism?', 1377. For a moderate and pragmatic defence of truth seeking as a justification for academic freedom, see Michael P. Lynch, 'Academic Freedom and the Politics of Truth', in Jennifer Lackey (ed.), *Academic Freedom,* Oxford University Press, Oxford, 2018.

[13]   *Abrams v United States,* 250 US 616, 630 (Holmes J) (1919).

[14]   Robert C Post, *Democracy, Expertise and Academic Freedom,* Yale University Press, New Haven, Ct, 2012, 63.

[15]   To borrow an expression from Michael P. Lynch, cited in Lackey, *Academic Freedom,* 26.

[16]   *Abrams v United States,* 250 US 616, 630 (Holmes J) (1919).

[17]   Allen Buchanan et al, *From Chance to Choice: Genetics and Justice* (Cambridge: Cambridge University Press, 2000); Allen Buchanan, 'Institutions, Beliefs and Ethics: Eugenics as a Case Study', *The Journal of Political Philosophy,* vol.15, 2007, 22.

[18]   See Mark Kelman, *A Guide to Critical Legal Studies,* Harvard University Press, Cambridge, Mass., 1987.

[19]   For an overview, see Kathryn Abrams, 'Hearing the Call of Stories', *California Law Review, vol.79,* 1991, 971.

[20]   Of course, journalists have *journalistic* expertise and a *journalistic* mission. These combine with their commitment to independence to justify press freedom but that is a separate from (and not inconsistent with) academic freedom.

[21]   J.S. Mill, On Liberty, ed. Elizabeth Rapaport, Hackett Publishing, Indianapolis, 1978, 52–54.

[22]   See William P. Marshall, 'The Truth Justification for Freedom of Speech', in Adrienne Stone and Frederick Schauer (eds), *The Oxford Handbook of Freedom of Speech,* Oxford University Press, Oxford, 2020.

[23]   R.L. Hasen, 'Cheap Speech and What It Has Done (to American Democracy)', *First Amendment Law Review,* vol.16, 2017, 200.

[24]   This argument operates cumulatively upon the argument that academic freedom pursues the advancement and dissemination of knowledge, but for those for whom doubts

about the possibility of advancing knowledge persist, it may provide a separate justification.

[25] See Ashutosh Bhagwat and James Weinstein, 'Freedom of Expression and Democracy', in Adrienne Stone and Frederick Schauer (eds), *The Oxford Handbook on Freedom of Speech*, Oxford University Press, Oxford, 2020.

[26] Many universities rely upon a link between education and the creation of citizens in their education mission statements. For example, the mission of Harvard College 'is to educate the citizen and citizen-leaders for our society'. 'Harvard at a Glance', Harvard University, 2019, www.harvard.edu/about-harvard/harvard-glance; see also Global Forum on Academic Freedom, Institutional Autonomy, and the Future of Democracy, 'Declaration', 21 June 2019, [1]. See further Andrew J. Perrin and Alanna

Gillis, 'How College Makes Citizens: Higher Education Experiences and Political Engagement' *Socius: Sociological Research for a Dynamic World,* vol.5, 2019, 1; Ceryn Evans, 'University Education Makes you a Better Citizen', *The Conversation,* 19 September 2017, https://theco nversation.com/university-educ ation-makes-you-a-better-citize n-83373; and this older but relevant study of the effect of educational attainment (from high school to university level) on political engagement: Kevin Milligan, Enrico Moretti and Philip Oreopoulos, 'Does Education Improve Citizenship? Evidence from the United States and the United Kingdom' *Journal of Public Economics,* vol.88, nos 9–10, 2004, 1667.

[27] On some accounts it is therefore essential for legitimate democratic government. Robert C Post, *Democracy, Expertise and Academic Freedom: A First*

Amendment Jurisprudence for the Modern State, Yale University Press, New Haven, Ct, 2012.

[28] Michael Ignatieff and Stefan Roch (eds), Academic Freedom: The Global Challenge (Budapest and New York: Central European University Press, 2018).

[29] Though in the United States, a court found that such a claim had no legal status in *Urofsky v Gilore* 216 F. 3d 401 (4th Cir. 2000).

[30] 'Academic Freedom', in Gary McCulloch and David Crook (eds), *The Routledge International Encyclopedia of Education* (London: Routledge, 2008).

[31] American Association of University Professors and Association of American Colleges, '1940 Statement of Principles on Academic Freedom and Tenure', AAUP, www.aaup.org/file/1940%20Statement.pdf.

[32]   The Independent Review's proposed definition of academic freedom includes the freedom of students to engage in intellectual inquiry, to express their views about the higher education provider in which they are enrolled, and to participate in student societies and associations. French, 'Report of the Independent Review', 226.

[33]   *Ridd v James Cook University* [2019] FCCA 997 (16 April 2019).

[34]   *Fair Work Act 2009* (Cth) s789FA-789FI.

[35]   Eric Barendt, *Academic Freedom and the Law: A Comparative Study,* Oxford: Hart Publishing, Oxford, 2010, 35–38; Robert C. Post, 'Discipline and Freedom in the Academy', *Arkansas Law Review,* vol.65, 2012, 204–05.

[36]   The American Association of University Professors, 'AAUP's 1915 Declaration of Principles', AAUP, www.aaup-ui.org/Docum ents/Principles/Gen_Dec_Princ.p

df.; Matthew W. Finkin and Robert C. Post, *For the Common Good: Principles of American Academic Freedom,* Yale University Press, New Haven, Ct, 2009, chapter 5; Rosalind Pritchard, 'Academic Freedom and Autonomy in the United Kingdom and Germany', *Minerva,* vol.36, no.2, Summer 1998, 101–24.

[37] Finkin and Post, *For the Common Good,* 23.

[38] Glyn Davis, *The Australian Idea of a University,* Melbourne University Press, Carlton, Vic., 2017, 34–42.

[39] Davis, *The Australian Idea of a University,* 42.

[40] Davis, *The Australian Idea of a University,* 42.

[41] University of Melbourne, 'Appropriate Workplace Behaviour Policy (MPF1328)', 8 November 2019, [5.1(a)].

[42] Deakin University, 'Code of Conduct', [6(a)].

[43]   University of Western Australia, 'Code of Ethics and Code of Conduct', January 2014, 7.

[44]   Flinders University, 'Social Media Guidelines', Flinders University, https://staff.flinders.edu.au/workplace-support/topic/social-media.

[45]   Comcare v Banerji [2019] HCA 23 (7 August 2019).

[46]   Elise Worthington, 'Murdoch University Drops Financial Claim against Whistleblower Academic after Backlash', ABC News, www.abc.net.au/news/2020-01-13 murdoch-university-drops-financial-claim-against-whistleblower/11863410.

[47]   French, 'Report of the Independent Review', 214–15.

[48]   For example, The University of Adelaide, 'Whistleblower Policy', 15 August 2017; Griffith University, 'Public Interest Disclosure Policy', 16 October 2018.

[49]   *Treasury Laws Amendment (Enhancing Whistleblower Protections) Act 2019* (Cth).

[50]   The American Association of University Professors, 'AAUP's 1915 Declaration of Principles', AAUP, www.aaup-ui.org/Docum ents/Principles/Gen_Dec_Princ.p df; see also their '1925 Conference Statement on Academic Freedom and Tenure' and '1940 Statement of Principles on Academic Freedom and Tenure', www.aaup.org/file /1940%20Statement.pdf.

[51]   Keith E. Whittington, 'Academic Freedom and the Scope of Protections for Extramural Speech', *Academe,* vol.105, no.1, 2019, 20, 25.

CHAPTER 4: FREEDOM OF SPEECH AND ITS LIMITS

[1]   Adrienne Stone, 'The Comparative Constitutional Law of Freedom of Expression' in Rosalind Dixon and Tom Ginsburg (eds), *Research Handbook on Comparative Constitutional Law,* Edward Elgar, Cheltenham, 2011.

[2]   Marshall 'The Truth Justification'; Catriona MacKenzie and Denise Meyerson, 'Autonomy and Free Speech' in Stone and Schauer, *The Oxford Handbook on Freedom of Speech;* Ashutosh Bhagwat and James Weinstein, 'Freedom of Expression and Democracy' in Stone and Schauer, *The Oxford Handbook on Freedom of Speech.*

[3]   S.G. Tallentyre (Evelyn Hall), *The Friends of Voltaire,* Smith Elder, London, 1906, 199.

[4]   *Palko v Connecticut* 302 U.S. 319, 327 (1937).

[5]   *West Virginia State Board of Education v Barnette* 319 U.S. 624, 642 (1943).

[6]   See Frederick Schauer, *Free Speech: A Philosophical Enquiry,* Cambridge University Press, New York 1982.

[7]   See Adrienne Stone, 'Expression', in Cheryl Saunders and Adrienne Stone (eds), *The Oxford Handbook of the Australian Constitution,* Oxford University Press, Oxford, 2018.

[8]   *Human Rights Act 2004* (ACT);
        *Victorian Charter of Rights and
        Responsibilities Act 2006* (Vic.);
        Human Rights Act 2019 (Qld).

[9]   *Ballina Shire Council v Ringland*
        (1994) 33 NSWLR 680 at 694
        and *New South Wales Aboriginal
        Land Council v Jones* (1998) 43
        NSWLR 300 provide illustrations.
        In these cases, the New South
        Wales Court of Appeal relied on
        freedom of speech as part of its
        reasoning that elected bodies like
        a shire council and an
        Indigenous land council could not
        sue for defamation. On
        interpreting statutes and
        regulations, see *Evans v New
        South Wales* (1998) 168 FCR
        576.

[10]   See Adrienne Stone, 'The Ironic
        Aftermath of *Eatock v Bolt'*,
        *Melbourne University Law
        Review,* vol.38, 2015, 926.

[11]   *Counter-Terrorism and Security
        Act 2015* (UK), s 26.

[12]   *Counter-Terrorism and Security
        Act 2015* (UK), s 31(2).

[13]   *Butt v Secretary of State for the Home Department* [2019] EWCA Civ 256 [177] (8 March 2019).

[14]   UK Government, 'Prevent Duty Guidance: For Higher Education Institutions in England and Wales', GOV.UK (website), April 2019, www.gov.uk/government /publications/prevent-duty-guid ance/prevent-duty-guidance-for -higher-education-institutions-in -england-and-wales.

[15]   Christopher McLeod, 'Mill on the Liberty of the Thought and Discussion', in Stone and Schauer, *The Oxford Handbook on Freedom of Speech.*

[16]   Stone, 'The Comparative Constitutional Law'.

[17]   The High Court of Australia has recognised limits on political communication for the prevention of obstruction of the Rundle Mall in Adelaide, see *Attorney-General (SA) v Corporation of the City of Adelaide* ('*Corneloup's Case*') (2013) 249 CLR 1; in

defamation cases see *Lange v Australian Broadcasting Corporation* (1997) 189 CLR 520; to protect protestors from physical harm see *Levy v Victoria* (1997) 189 CLR 520; and to prevent certain kinds of threats and harassment see *Monis v The Queen* (2013) 249 CLR 92.

[18] *Unions of New South Wales v New South Wales* (2013) 252 CLR 530.

[19] Alon Harel, 'Hate Speech', in Stone and Schauer, *The Oxford Handbook on Freedom of Speech.*

[20] Susan Svrluga, 'Duke Student Admitted Hanging Noose from Tree on Campus, School Officials Say', *The Washington Post,* 3 April 2015, www.washi ngtonpost.com/news/grade-poin t/wp/2015/04/02/duke-student-admitted-hanging-noose-from-t ree-on-campus-school-officials-s ay; Sigal Ben-Porath, *Free Speech on Campus,* University

of Pennsylvania Press, Pennsylvania, 2017, 65.

[21] Heidi Han, '"Kill Chinese" and Nazi Symbol Found Scrawled on Sydney Uni Grounds', *SBS,* 3 August 2017, www.sbs.com. au/language/english/kill-chinese -and-nazi-symbol-found-scrawle d-on-sydney-uni-grounds; Naaman Zhou, 'Holocaust Denial Leaflets at Australian Universities Spark Confrontation', *The Guardian,* 27 April 2017, www.theguardia n.com/australia-news/2017/apr /27/holocaust-denial-leaflets-at- australian-universities-spark-co nfrontation; Kathy Lord, 'Offensive Flyers Targeting Chinese Students Found at Melbourne Universities', *ABC News,* 26 July 2017, www.abc. net.au/news/2017-07-25/offens ive-flyers-removed-from-melbou rne-university-building/874182 0; Liam Donohoe, '"Stop the Asian Invasion": Racist Graffiti Appears on Campus', *Honi Soit,* 2 July 2018, https://honisoit.co

m/2018/07/stop-the-asian-inva
sion-racist-graffiti-appears-on-c
ampus.

[22]   *Toben v Jones* (2003) 129 FCR
515.

[23]   Rebecca Urban and Bernard
Lane, 'Feminists Reject
Transgender Law Change', *The
Australian,* 8 August 2019, ww
w.theaustralian.com.au/nation/f
eminists-reject-transgender-law
-change/news-story/b6b175fdd
e25714bbbd4f31ec63c2ac3;
Steven Morris, 'Germaine Greer
Gives University Lecture Despite
Campaign to Silence Her', *The
Guardian,* 19 November 2015,
www.theguardian.com/books/20
15/nov/18/transgender-activists
-protest-germaine-greer-lecture
-cardiff-university.

[24]   *Whitney v California* 274 US
357, 375 (1925).

[25]   'Those "Snowflakes"; Have
Chilling Effects Even Beyond the
Campus', *Wall Street Journal,*
21 April 2017, www.wsj.com/a
rticles/those-snowflakes-have-c

hilling-effects-even-beyond-the-campus-1492800913.

[26]   Frederick   Schauer,   'The Exceptional First Amendment', in M. Ignatieff (ed.), *American Exceptionalism and Human Rights,* Princeton University Press, Princeton, 2005.

[27]   Gallup Inc., *Free Speech on Campus: What College Students Think about First Amendment Issues,* Gallup Inc. and James L Knight Foundation and Newseum Institute, Washington, DC, 2017, https://knightfounda tion.org/wp-content/uploads/20 20/01/Knight_Foundation_Free_ Expression_on_Campus_2017.p df.

[28]   Kirstie Hewlett and Jonathan Grant, 'Freedom of Expression in UK Universities', December 2019, https://doi.org/10.6084/ m9.figshare.11108978.

[29]   Katharine Gelber and Luke McNamara, 'Evidencing the Harms of Hate Speech', *Social Identities, vol.*22, no.3, 2016, 324.

[30] Sigal Ben-Porath, *Free Speech on Campus,* University of Pennsylvania Press, Pennsylvania, 2017.

[31] *R v Butler* [1992] 1 SCR 452; *R v Keegstra* [1990] 3 SCR 697; Adrienne Stone, 'Canadian Constitutional Law and Freedom of Expression', in Richard Albert and David R. Cameron (eds), *Canada in the World: Comparative Perspectives on the Canadian Constitution,* Cambridge University Press, Cambridge, 2017, 245, 256.

[32] Jeremy Waldron, *The Harm in Hate Speech,* Harvard University Press, Cambridge, Mass., 2012.

[33] Ulrich Baer, *What Snowflakes Get Right: Free Speech, Truth and Equality on Campus,* Oxford University Press, Oxford, 2019.

[34] It was claimed that academic freedom justified the treatment of Indigenous human remains as scientific objects. See Paul Turnbull, *Science, Museums and Collecting the Indigenous Dead*

in Colonial Australia, Palgrave Macmillan, Cham, 2017.

[35] Scientist Lucky Tran has pointed out that the anti-vax movement use a strategy known as 'firehosing' – propagating many lies in a quantity so large that they are hard to fact check. The aim of this strategy is not to positively persuade the public in favour of a position, but to undermine established facts: Lucky Tran, 'Firehosing: The Systematic Strategy that Anti-Vaxxers Are Using to Spread Misinformation', *The Guardian,* 7 November 2019, www.theguardian.com/commentisfree/2019/nov/07/firehosing-the-systemic-strategy-that-anti-vaxxers-are-using-to-spread-misinformation. The harmful consequences of the anti-vax movement are falling rates of vaccination and increasing outbreaks of preventable and serious diseases such as measles: Ayelet Evrony and Arthur Caplan, 'The Overlooked

Dangers of Anti-Vaccination Groups' Social Media Presence', *Human Vaccines & Immunotherapeutics,* vol.13, no.6, 2017, 1475–76.

[36] Erwin Chemerinsky, 'False Speech and the First Amendment' *Oklahoma Law Review,* vol.71, no.1, 2018; Seana Shiffrin, *Speech Matters: On Lying, Morality and the Law,* Princeton University Press, Princeton, 2014, especially chapters 4 and 5.

[37] For example, Mark Schliebs, 'University of Melbourne to Host Foul-Mouthed Marxists' *The Australian,* 30 January 2020, w ww.theaustralian.com.au/higher -education/university-of-melbou rne-to-host-foulmouthed-marxis ts/news-story/f2322cfd51b199d cf111c04838897b02.

[38] Lee Bollinger, *The Tolerant Society,* Oxford University Press, Oxford, 1986.

[39] Helene Cooper, 'Ahmadinejad, at Columbia, Parries and Puzzles', *The New York Times,*

25 September 2007, www.nyti mes.com/2007/09/25/world/mi ddleeast/25iran.html; Office of the President Lee C. Bollinger, 'Statement about President Ahmadinejad's Scheduled Appearance', Columbia University, 19 September 2007, www.columbia.edu/cu/president /docs/communications/2007-20 08/070919-Statement-visit-Iran ian-President.html.

[40]   Equality and Human Rights Commission, 'Freedom of Expression: A Guide for Higher Education Providers and Students Unions in England and Wales', Equality and Human Rights Commission, London, February 2019, 33.

[41]   There can be very solid reasons for thinking that such disruption is likely when, for example, the same speaker or topic has created problems on other campuses. For example, the University of Michigan reportedly postponed and then cancelled an event that was

part of white nationalist Richard Spencer's college tour after his appearance at Michigan State University led to clashes between attendees and protesters and resulted in the arrest of twenty-five people. Luke Barnes, 'White Supremacist Richard Spencer Is Surprised His College Tour Was a Total Bust', *ThinkProgress*, 12 March 2018, https://thinkprogr ess.org/richard-spencer-college-tour-failure-535ddd203727.

[42] Harry Kalven, Jr, *The Negro and the First Amendment*, Ohio State University Press, Columbus, 1965, 140.

[43] Caroline Simon, 'Free Speech Isn't Free: It's Costing College Campuses Millions', *Forbes*, 20 November 2017, www.forbes.c om/sites/carolinesimon/2017/11 /20/free-speech-isnt-free-its-co sting-college-campuses-millions /#2088099b1ee7.

[44] University of Sydney Vice Chancellor Michael Spence has explained that the university's

policy is to charge event organisers for the cost of security. Michael Spence, 'Security the Only Cost in the Marketplace of Ideas', *The Australian,* 25 September 2018, www.theaustralian.com.au/commentary/opinion/security-the-only-cost-in-the-marketplace-of-ideas/news-story/863101b24337f80b5b78bb 68cb422c9d; Education Minister Dan Tehan proposed in September 2018 that protesters should have pay the cost of security at campus events: Michael Koziol, 'You Protest, You Pay: Education Minister's Bid to Bolster Free Speech at Universities', *The Sydney Morning Herald,* 22 September 2018, www.smh.com.au/politics/federal/you-protest-you-pay-education-minister-s-bid-to-bolster-free-speech-at-universities-20180921-p5057h.html.

[45]   French, 'Report of the Independent Review', March 2019. In the revised version,

cl. 6(e) allows for external speakers to be asked to pay the costs associated with security.

[46]   University of New South Wales, 'The Code of Conduct', 14 August 2017, Part B: Obligations, www.gs.unsw.edu.au/policy/documents/codeofconduct.pdf.

[47]   Murdoch University, 'Student Code of Conduct', 8 December 2010, 2, 3.2, www.murdoch.edu.au/School-of-Education/_document/MUSE-Documents/Student-Code-of-Conduct.pdf.

[48]   Sigal Ben-Porath, *Free Speech on Campus,* University of Pennsylvania Press, Pennsylvania, 2017, 71.

CHAPTER 5: EMERGING THREATS: FUNDING MODELS AND RESEARCH PARTNERSHIPS

[1]   Glyn Davis, *The Australian Idea of a University,* Melbourne

University Press, Carlton, Vic., 2017, 98. See also Simon Marginson and Mark Considine, *The Enterprise University: Power, Governance and Reinvention in Australia,* Cambridge University Press, Melbourne, 2000.

[2]   Australian Trade and Investment Commission, 'Education Data', w ww.austrade.gov.au/Australian/E ducation/Education-data/Current-data/summaries-and-news.

[3]   J.P. O'Neill, '1966 Census of Population and Housing Publications: Part 6 Educational Attainment', Commonwealth Bureau of Census and Statistics, Canberra, October 1970, 1, ww w.ausstats.abs.gov.au/ausstats/f ree.nsf/0/367A66778AE35ACBCA 25788000815CEC/$File/1966%20 Census%20-%20Volume%201%2 0Population%20-%20Single%20C haracteristics%20-%20Part%206 %20Educational%20Attainment.p df.

[4]   Australian Bureau of Statistics, 'Census of Population and Housing: Reflecting Australia –

Stories from the Census 2016', www.abs.gov.au/ausstats/abs@.n sf/Lookup/by%20Subject/2071.0 ~2016~Main%20Features~Educa tional%20Qualifications%20Data %20Summary%20~65.

[5] Australian Bureau of Statistics, Census of Population and Housing'.

[6] Department of Education, Skills and Employment, 'Finance Publication', Higher Education Publications, 2018, www.educati on.gov.au/finance-publication.

[7] Louise Bunce, Amy Baird and Sian E. Jones, 'The Student-as-Consumer Approach in Higher Education and Its Effect on Academic Performance', *Studies in Higher Education,* vol.52, no.11, 2017; Michael Tomlinson, 'Student Perceptions of Themselves as 'Consumers' of Higher Education', *British Journal of Sociology of Education* vol.38, no.4, 2017, 450–67. Bunce, Baird and Jones conclude that 'consumer orientation mediated traditional relationships between

learner identity, grade goal and academic performance'. Interestingly, they also find a link between consumer orientation and lower academic performance. Tomlinson concludes there is evidence that UK higher education students are increasingly identifying as consumers, but stresses that a variety of views towards higher education exist among students.

[8] Dr Paul Greatrix, 'University Isn't Just a Business – and the Student Isn't Always Right', The Guardian, 15 March 2011, www. theguardian.com/higher-educatio n-network/higher-education-netw ork-blog/2011/mar/14/students-as-consumers. In the US context: Tom Nichols, 'Don't Let Students Run the University' The Atlantic, 7 May 2019, www.thea tlantic.com/ideas/archive/2019/0 5/camille-paglia-protests-represe nt-dangerous-trend/588859.

[9] Catherine Bovill, Alison Cook-Sather and Peter Felten, 'Students as Co-Creators of

Teaching Approaches, Course Design and Curricula: Implications for Academic Developers', *International Journal for Academic Development,* vol.16, no.2, 2011, 133–45.

[10]   G r a n t   H a r m a n, 'Internationalisation of Australian Higher Education', in M. Tight (ed.), *International Relations: International Perspectives on Higher Education Research,* vol.3, Emerald Group Publishing Limited, Bingley, UK, 2005; Catriona Jackson, 'How International Students Benefit Australia', *Australian Financial Review,* 12 August 2018, www .afr.com/policy/health-and-educ ation/jackson-oped-20180812-h 13urj; Strategy Policy and Research in Education Ltd, 'The Nature of International Education in Australian Universities and its Benefits', report prepared for Universities Australia September 2009; M a r g a r e t   G a r d n e r,

'Internationalising Australian Higher Education', speech, Australian Institute of International Affairs, 11 October 2017.

[11] Sophie Arkoudis, 'Teaching International Students: Strategies to Enhance Learning', *report, Centre for the Study of Higher Education, University of Melbourne, 2006;* Carol S. Weinstein, Saundra Tomlinson-Clarke, Mary Curran, 'Towards a Conception of Culturally Responsive Classroom Management', *Journal of Teacher Education,* vol.5, no.1, 2004, 25–38.

[12] Primrose Riordan, 'Wrong Map Ignites University Fury', *The Australian,* 24 August 2017, w ww.theaustralian.com.au/nation al-affairs/sydney-lecturer-apolo gises-for-use-of-map-offending-chinese-students/news-story/2b 1cccbe438 d1c680fcbff60f8e7d9 7e, accessed 15 March 2019.

[13] Primrose Riordan, 'Monash Throws out the Textbook over

Chinese Student Complaints', *The Australian,* 30 May 2017, www.theaustralian.com.au/higher-education/monash-throws-out-the-textbook-over-chinese-student-complaints/news-story/3453651355ed61ab28989e7623c8dd9d.

[14]   Primrose Riordan, 'Monash Throws out the Textbook'; Matthew Lesh, 'Australia's Universities Are Failing to Protect Free Speech' *ABC News,* 3 October 2017, www.abc.net.au/news/2017-10-03/australias-universities-are-failing-to-protest-free-speech/9007346.

[15]   Primrose Riordan and Rowan Callick, 'China Consulate Involved in Newcastle Uni Taiwan Row', *The Australian,* 28 August 2017, www.theaustralian.com.au/national-affairs/china-consulate-involved-in-newcastle-uni-taiwan-row/news-story/14dceb31c1e72807c9f006936784c601.

[16] Riordan and Callick, 'China Consulate Involved in Newcastle Uni Taiwan Row'.

[17] YouTube, 'Indian Lecturer Saying Taiwan Is a Separate Country', 22 August 2017, www.youtube.com/watch?v=T6vcsMm_Al8&feature=youtu.be; Primrose Riordan and Rowan Callick, 'China Consulate Involved in Newcastle Uni Taiwan Row' *The Australian,* 28 August 2017, www.theaustralian.com.au/national-affairs/china-consulate-involved-in-newcastle-uni-taiwan-row/news-story/14dceb31c1e72807c9f006936784c601.

[18] Gwyneth Ho, 'Why Australian Universities Have Upset Chinese Students' *BBC News,* 5 September 2017, www.bbc.com/news/world-australia-41104634.

[19] Primrose Riordan, 'Wrong Map Ignites Fury' *The Australian,* 24 August 2017, www.theaustralian.com.au/nation/politics/sydney-lecturer-apologises-for-use-of-

map-offending-chinese-students
/news-story/2b1cccbe438d1c68
0fcbff60f8e7d97e.

[20] Riordan, 'Wrong Map Ignites Fury'.

[21] Clive Hamilton, *Silent Invasion*, Hardie Grant, Richmond, Vic., 2018, 165.

[22] Fergus Hunter, 'A Student Attended a Protest at an Australian Uni. Days later Chinese Officials Visited His Family' The *Sydney Morning Herald,* 7 August 2019, www.s mh.com.au/politics/federal/this-student-attended-a-protest-at-a n-australian-uni-days-later-chin ese-officials-visited-his-family-2 0190807-p52eqb.html; Naaman Zhou and Ben Smee, '"We Cannot Be Seen": The Fallout from the University of Queensland's Hong Kong Protests', *The Guardian,* 4 August 2019, www.theguardian .com/australia-news/2019/aug/ 04/we-cannot-be-seen-the-fallo ut-from-the-university-of-queen slands-hong-kong-protests.

[23]   Human Rights Watch, 'Resisting Chinese Efforts to Undermine Academic Freedom: A Code of Conduct for Colleges, Universities and Academic Institutions Worldwide', report, 21 March 2019, www.hrw.org/ sites/default/files/supporting_re sources/190321_china_academi c_freedom_coc_0.pdf.

[24]   Human Rights Watch, 'Resisting Chinese Efforts to Undermine Academic Freedom'.

[25]   To be classified as an 'Australian University', an institution must undertake 'research that leads to the creation of new knowledge and original creative endeavour'. Higher Education Standards Framework (Threshold Standards) 2015 B1.1(2)).

[26]   Jon Piccini and Dirk Moses, 'Simon Birmingham's Intervention in Research Funding Is Not Unprecedented, But Dangerous' *The Conversation*, 26 October 2018, https://theconversation.com/sim

on-birminghams-intervention-in
-research-funding-is-not-unprec
edented-but-dangerous-105737.
See also Gideon Haig, 'The
Nelson Touch: Research Funding
The New Censorship', *The
Monthly,* May 2006, 20.

[27] It is usually traced to
recommendations of Lord
Haldane in the 'Report of the
Machinery of Government
Committee 1918' ('Haldane
Report'), Ministry of
Reconstruction, London, 1918,
but may in fact be attributable
to later interpretations of those
recommendations. See David
Edgerton 'Haldane Principle's
"Centenary" Is a Good Time to
Bury Its Myth', *Research
Fortnight,* 2018.

[28] 'Data Snapshot 2018',
Universities Australia, 5
February 2018, 33.

[29] Department of Education, Skills
and Employment, 'Research
Income Data (2004–2018)', 18
December 2019, https://docs.e
ducation.gov.au/node/47851.

[30]   'Eradicating Cervical Cancer', Uniquest, https://uniquest.com.au/impact_stories/a-global-solution-to-eradicating-cervical-cancer.

[31]   University of Queensland, 'UQ Responds', *UQ News,* www.uq.edu.au/news/uq-responds.

[32]   For instance, see 'UNSW Confronts the Greatest Issues Facing Humanity by Leading Research, Policy and Public Conversations that Can Change the World', Grand Challenges, https://grandchallenges.unsw.edu.au; H.W. Rittel and M.M. Webber, 'Dilemmas in a General Theory of Planning', *Policy Sciences,* vol.4, no.2, 1973, 155–69.

[33]   See, for example, Ministers for the Department of Education (Cth), 'Greater Collaboration between Universities and Business', media release, 16 December 2019, https://ministers.education.gov.au/tehan/greater-collaboration-between-universities-and-business.

[34] Tony Klein, 'The Value of Fundamental Inquiry: The View from Physics', in Tony Coady (ed.), *Why Universities Matter: A Conversation about Values, Means and Directions,* Allen & Unwin, Sydney, 2000, 99–100.

[35] Klaus Lieb and Armin Scheurich, 'Contact between Doctors and the Pharmaceutical Industry, Their Perceptions, and the Effects on Prescribing Habits' *PLOS ONE,* vol.9, no.10, 2014.

[36] For example, in Australia the Minderoo Foundation supports initiatives in areas including early childhood development ('Thrive by Five'), ending modern slavery ('Walk Free') and ending the disparity between Indigenous and non-Indigenous Australians ('Generation One'). See The Minderoo Foundation website (www.minderoo.com.au). The Ian Potter Foundation supports initiatives in areas including early childhood development, community wellbeing,

homelessness and Indigenous health. See the Ian Potter Foundation website (www.ianpotter.org.au/what-we-support).

[37] For an overview, see Mark Dodgson, 'How Philanthropy Could Change Higher Education' *The Conversation,* 1 March 2018, https://theconversation.com/how-philanthropy-could-change-higher-education-funding-92260.

[38] 'Creating Employment Parity with and for Indigenous Australians', Minderoo Foundation website, accessed 10 December 2020, www.minderoo.org/generation-one; Paul Ramsay Foundation website, accessed 10 December 2020, https://paulramsayfoundation.org.au; 'What We Support', Ian Potter Foundation website, www.ianpotter.org.au/what-we-support.

[39] 'About Us', the Ramsay Centre website, www.ramsaycentre.org/about-us/frequently-asked-questions.

[40] Tellingly, conservatives and progressives accused each other of reigniting the culture war: Robert Bolton, 'Culture Wars Back as Academics Reject "Ideological" Course' *The Australian Financial Review,* 11 April 2019, https://www.afr.com/policy/health-and-education/culture-wars-back-as-academics-reject-ideological-course-20190410-p51cwz; Sam Brennan, 'The Australian Starts a New Culture War over the Ramsay Centre and Threatens Academic Freedom', *Independent Australia,* 1 July 2018, https://independentaustralia.net/business/business-display/the-australian-misreports-ramsay-centre-for-western-civilisation-firestorm-,11651.

[41] On the agreement with the University of Queensland, see 'Frequently Asked Questions', The University of Queensland, 2019, https://staff.uq.edu.au/update/projects-initiatives/ramsay-centre-partnership/faq.

[42]   'Frequently Asked Questions' ('How Will UQ Maintain Its Academic Independence?').

[43]   Business Council of Australia, 'Australians Deserve More from Their Post-Secondary Education and Skills System', media release, 1 March 2019, https://www.bca.com.au/australians_deserve_more_from_their_post_secondary_education_and_skills_system; Nick Wailes, 'Why Universities Need to Respond More Quickly to Business Demand' *The Australian Financial Review,* 18 November 2018, https://www.afr.com/policy/health-and-education/why-universities-need-to-respond-more-quickly-to-business-demand-nick-wailes-20181116-h17z5f.

[44]   National Health and Medical Research Council and Australian Research Council and Universities Australia, 'Australian Code for the Responsible Conduct of Research, 2018', report, 2018, Preamble, 1, https://www.nhmrc.gov.au/about-

us/publications/australian-code-responsible-conduct-research-2018.

[45]   National Health and Medical Research Council, Australian Research Council and Universities Australia, 'Disclosure of Interests and Management of Conflicts of Interests: A Guide Supporting the Australian Code for the Responsible Conduct of Research', report, 2019, https://www.nhmrc.gov.au/file/14503/download?token=lixhoic2.

[46]   Adrian Pokomy, 'Why We Need to Pay More Attention to Negative Clinical Trials', *The Conversation,* 9 June 2016, https://theconversation.com/why-we-need-to-pay-more-attention-to-negative-clinical-trials-59904. The author also notes, however, that it is mainly the 'game changer' positive outcomes that garner media and public attention; Tom Reynolds, 'Eliminating Publication Bias: The Effect of

Negative Trial Results', *Journal of the National Cancer Institute,* vol.92, no.9, 2000, 682, https://academic.oup.com/jnci/article/92/9/682/2906116.

[47]   L.B. Strand, P. Clark, N. Graves et al, 'Time to Publication for Publicly Funded Clinical Trials in Australia: An Observational Study', *BMJ Open,* vol.7, 2017, https://bmjopen.bmj.com/content/7/3/e012212.

[48]   World Health Organization, 'WHO Statement on Public Disclosure of Clinical Trial Results', World Health Organization, April 2015, www.who.int/ictrp/results/WHO_Statement_results_reporting_clinical_trials.pdf?ua=1; 'All Trials', www.alltrials.net.

[49]   Nola M. Ries and Kypros Kypri, 'Government-Funded Health Research Contracts in Australia: A Critical Assessment of Transparency', *Sydney Law Review,* vol.40, no.3, 2018: 367; Georgia Clark, 'Research Freedom Undermined by

Government Contracts', *Government News,* 21 January 2019, https://www.government news.com.au/research-freedom -undermined-by-government-co ntracts.

[50] Camron Slessor, 'Student Activists Rally against "weapons research" at Adelaide University', *ABC News,* 10 October 2018, https://www.abc .net.au/news/2018-10-10/union -joins-fight-against-militarisatio n-of-university/10356886; Henrietta Cook and Education Editor, 'Students Angry about Missile-Maker Lockheed Martin's Lab at Melbourne University' *The Age,* 26 September 2016, https://www.theage.com.au/nat ional/victoria/students-angry-ab out-missilemaker-lockheed-mar tins-lab-at-melbourne-university -20160926-grorqj.html.

CHAPTER 6: FOSTERING OPEN MINDS: SOME PRACTICAL OPTIONS

[1]	Institute of Public Affairs, 'Free Speech on Campus Audit 2017', report, December 2017, 2, https://ipa.org.au/wp-content/uploads/2017/12/IPA-Report-Free-Speech-on-Campus-Audit-2017.pdf; Jeremy Sammut, 'University Freedom Charters: How to Best Protect Free Speech on Australian Campuses', *Policy Paper,* no.10, October 2018; Augusto Zimmerman, 'Why We Need a Chicago Statement', Quadrant, 26 February 2019, https://quadrant.org.au/opinion/qed/2019/02/why-we-need-a-chicago-statement.

[2]	Dan Tehan, 'Review into University Freedom of Speech', media release, 14 November 2018, https://ministers.dese.gov.au/tehan/review-university-freedom-speech.

[3] Committee on Freedom of Expression at the University of Chicago, 'Report of the Committee on Freedom of Expression', University of Chicago, 2014, https://provost.u chicago.edu/sites/default/files/do cuments/reports/FOECommitteeR eport.pdf.

[4] Committee on Freedom of Expression, 'Report of the Committee'.

[5] Foundation for Individual Rights in Education, 'Chicago Statement: University and Faculty Body Support', FIRE, 6 February 2020, https://www.thefire.org/chicago-statement-university-and-faculty-body-support.

[6] 376 US 254, 270 (1964).

[7] Vincent Blasi, 'The First Amendment and the Ideal of Civic Courage', *William and Mary Law Review,* vol.29, 1988, 653; Vincent Blasi, 'The Pathological Perspective and the First Amendment'. *Columbia Law Review,* vol.85, 1985, 449.

[8]   Frederick   Schauer,   'The
        Exceptional First Amendment', in
        M.   Ignatieff   (ed.),   *American*
        Exceptionalism   and   Human
        Rights,   Princeton   University
        Press, Princeton, 2005, 29–56.
[9]   Schauer, 'The Exceptional First
        Amendment', 29–56.
[10]   Schauer, 'The Exceptional First
        Amendment', 29–56.
[11]   *Citizens   United*   v.   *Federal*
        Election Commission, 558 U.S.
        310 (2010); *R.A.V. v.* City of
        St. Paul, 505 U.S. 377 (1992).
[12]   Columbia   Law   Review
        Association, 'Symposium: A
        First Amendment for All? Free
        Expression   in   an   Age   of
        Inequality',   *Columbia   Law*
        Review, vol.118, 2018, 7.
[13]   Adrienne   Stone,   'The
        Comparative Constitutional Law
        of Freedom of Expression', in
        Rosalind   Dixon   and   Tom
        Ginsburg   (eds),   *Research*
        Handbook   on   Comparative
        Constitutional   Law,   Edward
        Elgar, Cheltenham, UK, 2011;
        Dieter   Grimm,   'Dignity',   in

Adrienne Stone and Frederick Schauer (eds), *The Oxford Handbook on Freedom of Speech,* Oxford University Press, Oxford, 2020.

[14]   University of Toronto Governing Council, 'Statement on Freedom of Speech', University of Toronto Secretariat, 28 May 1992, https://governingcouncil. utoronto.ca/secretariat/policies/ freedom-speech-statement-may -28-1992.

[15]   University of Toronto Governing Council, 'Statement on Equity, Diversity, and Excellence', University of Toronto Secretariat, 14 December 1992, https://governingcouncil.utoron to.ca/sites/default/files/2019-12 /equitydiversity%20%20statem ent%20on%20equity%2C%20di versity%20and%20excellence.p df.

[16]   We note that the University of Toronto has retained its longstanding statement, even after the imposition of a requirement by the Ontario

government that all colleges and universities develop a free speech policy including principles based on the University of Chicago Statement. Office of the Premier, 'Upholding Free Speech on Ontario's University and College Campuses', media release, 30 April 2018, cited in Robert French, 'Report of the Independent Review of Freedom of Speech in Australian Higher Education Providers', Department of Education and Training, Canberra, 2019, 77–78.

[17]   French, 'Report of the Independent Review', 99.

[18]   French, 'Report of the Independent Review', 230, 235.

[19]   French, 'Report of the Independent Review', 232–33.

[20]   French, 'Report of the Independent Review', 235.

[21]   French, 'Report of the Independent Review', 236.

[22]   Scott Jaschik, 'The Chicago Letter and Its Aftermath',

Inside Higher Education, website, 29 August 2016, https://www.insidehighered.com/news/2016/08/29/u-chicago-letter-new-students-safe-spaces-sets-intense-debate.

[23]   The University of Chicago tells incoming freshmen it does not support 'trigger warnings' or 'safe spaces'. John Ellison, Letter from the Office of the Dean of Students to the Class of 2020 Students, 2020, https://news.uchicago.edu/sites/default/files/attachments/Dear_Class_of_2020_Students.pdf.

[24]   Karin Deist, 'Eisgruber Selects Book on Free Speech and Universities for Pre-Read', Princeton University Office of Communications, 7 February 2018, www.princeton.edu/news/2018/02/07/eisgruber-selects-book-free-speech-and-universities-pre-read.

APPENDIX A: A SUMMARY OF THE 'REPORT OF THE

INDEPENDENT REVIEW OF FREEDOM OF SPEECH IN AUSTRALIAN HIGHER EDUCATION PROVIDERS'

[1]   Dan Tehan, 'Independent Review of Freedom of Speech in Australian Higher Education Providers', media release, 6 April 2019, https://ministers.dese.gov.au/tehan/independent-review-freedom-speech-australian-higher-education-providers-0.

[2]   Robert French, 'Report of the Independent Review of Freedom of Speech in Australian Higher Education Providers', Department of Education and Training, Canberra, 2019, 13.

[3]   French, 'Report of the Independent Review', 14.

[4]   French, 'Report of the Independent Review', 14.

[5]   French, 'Report of the Independent Review', 18.

[6]   French, 'Report of the Independent Review', 18.

[7]   French, 'Report of the Independent Review', 18.

[8]   French, 'Report of the Independent Review', 18, 20.

[9]   Employment, Workplace Relations, Small Business and Education References Committee, 'Universities in Crisis', The Committee, Parliament of the Commonwealth of Australia, Canberra, 2001.

[10]   French, 'Report of the Independent Review', 31, 32.

[11]   French, 'Report of the Independent Review', 37.

[12]   French, 'Report of the Independent Review', 224.

[13]   French, 'Report of the Independent Review', 225.

[14]   French, 'Report of the Independent Review', 225.

APPENDIX B: A CRITICAL REVIEW OF THE INSTITUTE FOR PUBLIC AFFAIRS' 'FREE

SPEECH ON CAMPUS AUDIT 2018'

[1]   Matthew Lesh, 'Free Speech on Campus Audit 2018', Institute of Public Affairs, Melbourne, December 2018, 2.

[2]   Lesh, 'Free Speech on Campus Audit 2018', 2, 4.

[3]   Lesh, 'Free Speech on Campus Audit 2018', 69.

[4]   Lesh, 'Free Speech on Campus Audit 2018', 2.

[5]   Commonwealth, *Parliamentary Debates,* House of Representatives, 26 May 2011, 4772 (Peter Garrett).

[6]   Lesh, 'Free Speech on Campus Audit 2018', 11.

[7]   Glyn Davis, 'Special Pleading: Free Speech and Australian Universities' *The Conversation,* 4 December 2018.

[8]   Lesh, 'Free Speech on Campus Audit 2018', 15.

[9]   Lesh, 'Free Speech on Campus Audit 2018', 15.

[10]   Lesh, 'Free Speech on Campus Audit 2018', 19.

Carolyn Evans is the vice-chancellor and president of Griffith University. Previously, she was the deputy vice-chancellor of the University of Melbourne and the dean of Melbourne Law School. An internationally recognised expert on religious freedom and human rights, Carolyn is the author of *Religious Freedom under the European Court of Human Rights, Australian Bills of Rights* and *The Legal Protection of Religious Freedom in Australia.* She is the coeditor of *Religion and International Law, Mixed Blessings* and *Law and Religion in Historical and Theoretical Perspective.*

Adrienne Stone holds a chair at Melbourne Law School, where she is also a Kathleen Fitzpatrick Australian Laureate Fellow, a Redmond Barry Distinguished Professor and the director of the Centre for Comparative Constitutional Studies. She is president of the International Association of Constitutional Law and an elected fellow of the Academy of Social Sciences in Australia and the Australian Academy of Law. Adrienne has published widely in international journals and is the coeditor of *The Oxford Handbook on the Australian Constitution* and *The Oxford Handbook on Freedom of Speech*.

BACK COVER MATERIAL

A CRISP, TIMELY AND DEFINITIVE LOOK AT THE COMPLEX TOPIC OF FREEDOM IN AUSTRALIAN UNIVERSITIES

Recently the alarm has been raised – basic freedoms are under attack in our universities. A generation of 'snowflake' students are shutting out ideas that challenge their views. Ideologically motivated academics are promoting propaganda at the expense of rigorous research and balanced teaching. Universities are caving in and denying platforms to 'problematic' public speakers. Is this true, or is it panic and exaggeration?

Carolyn Evans and Adrienne Stone deftly investigate the arguments, analysing recent controversies and delving into the history of the university. They consider the academy's core values and purpose, why it has historically given higher protection to certain freedoms, and how competing legal, ethical and practical claims can restrict free expression.

This book asks the necessary questions and responds with thoughtful, reasoned answers. Are universities responsible for helping students to thrive in a free intellectual climate? Are public figures who work outside of academia owed an audience? Does a special duty of care exist for students and faculty targeted by hostile speech? And are high-profile cases diverting attention from more complex, serious threats to freedom in universities – such as those posed by domestic and foreign governments, industry partners and donors?

A

1915 'Declaration on Principles of Academic Freedom and Tenure', *103, 105, 161*

'1940 Statement of Principles on Academic Freedom and Tenure', *105, 135, 136*

1967 referendum, *56*

see also Indigenous-rights activism,

academic freedom, *4, 50, 51, 62, 64, 67, 71, 73, 74, 76, 77, 79, 98, 103, 105, 107, 139, 156, 161, 165, 170, 183, 207, 209, 255, 257, 258*

see also enterprise agreements; Independent

Review; John Stuart Mill,

and academic disputes, *148, 150, 151, 153, 155*

in the classroom, *135, 136, 142, 144*

and debate, *4, 58, 87, 144, 148, 207, 237*

and democracy, *127, 129, 131*

as distinct from freedom of speech, *73, 87, 109, 111, 140, 144, 146, 252*

'extramural expression', *158*

and freedom to learn (lernfreiheit), *131, 133, 135*

institutional freedom, *136, 139*

interference from foreign governments, *139, 211, 214, 216*

interference from government, *6, 8, 9, 15, 20, 22, 27, 33, 34, 58, 218, 220*

'intramural expression', *151*

the Model Code, *94, 96, 98*

policies in support of, *81, 83, 85*

and public expression, *144, 146, 148, 150, 151, 153, 155, 156, 158, 161*

see also 'extramural expression'; 'intramural expression',

and the pursuit of knowledge, *116, 118, 121, 122, 124, 126, 127, 131, 133, 135, 146, 151, 185*

'Report of the Independent Review of Freedom of Speech in Australian Higher Education Providers', *100, 101*

and research, *71, 73, 81, 83, 109, 116, 122, 124, 131, 133, 146, 148, 207, 214*

and teaching, *131, 133, 135, 139, 146, 148, 150, 165*

academics, *6, 37, 115, 127, 161, 186*

see also research; researchers; teaching,

civility, *79, 101, 148, 150, 155, 193, 243*

the Model Code, *94, 96*

and public expression, *144, 146, 148, 150, 151, 153, 155, 156, 158, 161*

pursuit of knowledge, *116, 118,*

121, 122, 124, 126, 127, 131, 133, 135, 146, 151, 185
research expertise, *121, 124, 151, 161, 218*
self-censorship, *27*
surveillance of, *8, 9, 17, 18, 20, 22, 24, 33, 34*
and university governance, *146, 150, 151, 153, 155, 156, 158*
activism, *47, 55, 56*
see also student protests,
Agar, W.E. (former professor at University of Melbourne), *4*
see also Farrago,
Ahmadinejad, Mahmoud (former president of Iran), *188*
American Association of University Professors (AAUP), *103, 105, 107, 135, 136, 161*
see also 1915 'Declaration on Principles of Academic Freedom and Tenure'; '1940 Statement of Principles on Academic Freedom and Tenure'; Association of American Colleges,
American civil-rights movement, *55, 56*
Anderson, Fay (media historian), *18, 31, 34*
Anderson, John (former professor at Sydney University), *24, 25, 27*
see also University of Sydney,
Andrew, R.R. (former

vice-chancellor of Monash University), *47*

anti-discrimination laws, *216*

apartheid, *55, 60*

ASIO,
see Australian Security Intelligence Organisation (ASIO),

Askin, Robert (former premier of New South Wales), *51*

Association of American Colleges, *105*
see also ' 1940 Statement of Principles on Academic Freedom and Tenure'; American Association of University Professors (AAUP),

atheism, *27*

Australian Anti-War League, *8*

Australian Capital Territory, *168*

Australian Code for Responsible Conduct of Research 2018, *233, 235*

Australian Constitution, *167, 168*

Australian Council for Civil Liberties, *31*

Australian Labor Party, *6, 9, 47, 53*

Australian National University (ANU), *18*
see also Charles Spry,

Australian Research Council, *113, 218, 220*

Australian Security Intelligence Organisation (ASIO), *17, 18, 20, 31* see also Australian National University (ANU); Charles Spry; Douglas Copland (former ANU vice-chancellor),

Australian Student Labour Federation, 46, 47

Australian Student Labour Federation Conference 1965, 46

Australian universities, 37, 46, 62, 64, 66, 67, 76, 77, 90, 100, 101, 103, 113, 214, 218, 233, 235

see also academics; research; researchers; teaching; student protests,

and advancement of knowledge, 253

as centres of political and cultural change, 37

codes of conduct, 85, 87, 88, 153, 155, 192, 193, 233, 235

Commonwealth grants, 22, 201, 207

culture of, 161, 241, 255

and debate, 4, 6, 8, 9, 11, 12, 15, 24, 34, 38, 50, 58, 77, 79, 85, 87, 88, 94, 188, 190, 198, 211

and enterprise agreements, 77, 79, 81, 83, 85

governance of, 41, 50, 146, 150, 151, 153, 156, 158, 255

institutional autonomy, 20, 22, 92, 136, 139, 218, 231

interference from governments, 6, 8, 15, 17, 18, 33, 34, 58, 214, 216

and international students, 198, 200, 201, 204, 207, 209, 211, 214, 216

internationalisation of teaching and research, *207, 209*
the learning environment, *205, 207*
and the Model Code, *94, 96, 98, 239, 243, 244, 250, 252*
and the political left, *6, 12, 17, 22, 33, 34, 58*
and the political right, *6, 47, 60*
selection-committee prejudice, *29, 34*
and 'subversive intellectuals', *18, 20*
the university community, *257, 258*

B
Bacon, Francis, *223*
Baxter, Philip (former Sydney University of Technology vice-chancellor), *29, 31*

BBC News, *214*
Ben-Porath, Sigal (Free Speech on Campus), *193*
Birmingham, Simon (former education minister), *218*
Boer War, *8*
Bollinger, Lee (Columbia University president), *188*
Bond University, *85, 87*
Brandeis, Louis (former US Supreme Court justice), *176*
Brennan, William J., Jr (former US Supreme Court justice) (New York Times Co. v Sullivan), *244*
Brenner, Y.S. (Dutch economist), *34*
see also University of

Adelaide; University of New South Wales, British University Grants Committee, 22

C

Cain, John (former premier of Victoria), 17

Cairns, Jim (former Labor MP), 20

Calwell, Arthur (former Labor Party leader), 55

Cambridge University, 12, 113, 151

Campion Society, 9, 11, 12

'Campus Free Speech Acts', 107

Canada, 98, 101, 103
  see also University of Toronto; Wilfrid Laurier University,

Ontario's free speech policies, 103

Canada Supreme Court, 181

Canberra University conduct and values charter, 88

Cardozo, Benjamin N. (former US Supreme Court justice), 165

Central European University, 131

Central Queensland University Enterprise Agreement 2017, 79, 81

Centre for Independent Studies, 239
  see also James Paterson,

Charles Darwin University, 87

Chicago Principles ('Report of the Committee on

Freedom of Expression'), *88, 103, 105, 107, 239, 241, 243, 244, 246, 250, 255, 257*
  see also University of Chicago,
Chicago Statement, see Chicago Principles,
Childe, Vere Gordon, *8, 9*
  see also Department of Defence; pacificism; Queen's College, Oxford; socialism; University of Sydney,
China, *200, 211, 214, 216*
China consulate-general, *211, 214*
Clark, Manning, *11*
Cold War, *17, 31, 37, 58*
Columbia University, *37, 43, 188*
  leadership, *188*

protests 1967, *37, 43*
  School of International and Public Affairs, *188*
Committee on Australian Universities 1957, *22*
common-law right, *168*
Commonwealth Department of National Services, *38*
Commonwealth Grant Scheme, *201*
Commonwealth legislation, *62, 64*
communism, *8, 9, 15, 18, 22, 24, 27, 31, 33, 34, 37*
  see also Cold War,
Communist Party of Australia, *4, 15, 20, 29, 31, 33, 34*
conscientious objectors, *46*

conscription, 6, 8, 46, 47, 50, 55

Copland, Douglas (former ANU vice-chancellor), 18

COVID-19 pandemic, 129, 196, 209

Crawford, Raymond Maxwell (historian), 31, 33, 34
see also Australian Council for Civil Liberties; University of Melbourne; University of Sydney,

Crowley, Frank (historian), 29

CSL Ltd, 222

Curthoys, Ann (historian and SAFA member), 56

Curtin University research management policy, 88

D

Davis, Glyn, 196, 198

Deakin University code of conduct, 153

debate, 4, 6, 8, 9, 11, 12, 24, 34, 50, 58, 85, 87, 88, 94, 100, 101, 105, 109, 142, 144, 148, 163, 165, 167, 174, 190, 198, 207, 211, 237, 241, 244, 248
see also public debate,
and academic freedom, 4, 58, 87, 144, 148, 207, 237
and Australian universities, 4, 6, 8, 9, 11, 12, 15, 24, 34, 38, 50, 58, 77, 79, 85, 87, 88, 94, 188, 190, 198, 211
and freedom of speech, 58, 88, 94, 100, 101, 163, 165, 167, 174, 181
Spanish Civil War debate 1937, 9, 11, 12

Deery, Phillip (Cold War historian), 29, 31

Defence Force Protection Act 1967 (Cth), *47*

democracy, *24, 127, 129, 131, 163, 172, 244, 248*

democratic nations, *109*

democratic reform, *43*

democratic rights, *181*

democratic system, *47*

Department of Aboriginal Affairs, *56*

Department of Defence, *9*

Department of Labour and National Service, *46, 50*

E

Edmunds, F.L. ('The Fight for World Supremacy' lecture), *33*

Education Act 1989 (NZ), *74, 76*

see also New Zealand,

Education Reform Act 1988 (UK), *74, 76*

see also United Kingdom,

Ellison, John (dean of students, College of University of Chicago), *255, 257*

enterprise agreements, *73, 77, 79, 81, 94, 155, 244*

see also Central Queensland University Enterprise Agreement 2017 Fair Work Commission; James Cook University Enterprise Agreement 2013-2016,

Equality and Human Rights, Commission (UK), *100, 190*

see also United
Kingdom,
'extramural
expression', 158

F
Fair Work
Commission, 77
Faraday, Michael,
223
Farrago, 2, 4, 11
fascism, 8, 9, 15
see also Full
Court of the
Federal Court,
First Amendment to
the Constitution of
the United States of
America, 239, 244, 246,
248
see also United
States,
Fish, Stanley
(literary theorist),
116
Flinders University,
50, 87
social media
guidelines, 153

Frazer, Ian
(Queensland
University
professor), 222
free intellectual
inquiry, 62, 64, 66, 67, 69,
71, 73, 76, 77, 90, 92, 109
see also
intellectual
inquiry,
free speech,
see freedom of
speech,
Free Speech
Movement 1964, 43
see also
University of
California,
'Free Speech on
Campus Audit
2018', 6
see also Institute
of Public Affairs,
Free Speech on
Campus (Sigal
Ben-Porath), 193
freedom of speech,
4, 6, 11, 12, 15, 17, 24, 25, 27,
42, 58, 60, 62, 64, 67, 71, 73, 76,

85, 94, 100, 107, 109, 116, 124, 177, 188, 193, 198, 209, 255, 257, 258

  see also John Stuart Mill,

  absolutist view of, 163, 165

  and academic freedom, 87

  on campus, 168

  in the classroom, 140, 142

  common-law right, 168

  in constitutional law, 172

  'crisis' of, 60, 88, 107

  debate, 58, 88, 94, 100, 101, 163, 165, 167, 174, 181

  and democracy, 127, 163, 172, 244, 248

  distinct from academic freedom, 73, 87, 109, 140, 144, 146

  and equality, 250

  expression of false ideas, 183, 185

First Amendment law (US), 244, 246, 248

  and harmful speech, 174, 176, 177, 180, 181, 183, 190, 192

  intellectual integrity, 183, 185

  interference from governments, 6, 8, 9, 34, 58, 211, 214

  international students, 214, 216

  and the legal system, 167, 168, 174, 176, 177, 181

  liberal theory of freedom of expression, 170, 172

  limitations of, 92, 165, 167, 170, 172

  the Model Code, 94, 96, 252, 253, 255

  protection of, 6, 87, 88, 90, 94, 96, 98, 101, 103, 105, 146, 172, 174

  in the 'public square', 96, 98, 167, 168, 185, 186, 188, 190, 192, 244, 252, 253 right to, *158, 161*

self-censorship, *27, 214*

the 'snowflake' objection, *176, 177, 180*

university policies on, *193, 194*

French, Robert (former chief justice of the High Court of Australia), *60, 62, 88, 90, 92, 94, 250*

  see also Independent Review; Model Code; 'Report of the Independent Review of Freedom of Speech in Australian Higher Education Providers'; University of Western Australia,

Full Court of the Federal Court, *73, 74, 155*

G

Galileo Galilei, *223*

Gardasil, *222*

Gardner, Margaret (Monash University vice-chancellor), *209*

Garrett, Peter (former education minister), *64, 71*

Gazette (Melbourne University publication), *17*

German universities, *151*

GlaxoSmithKline PLC, *222*

Gorton government, *46*

H

Haldane Principle, *218*

  see also United Kingdom,

Hamilton, Clive, *53*

Hartwell, Max (Sydney University of Technology), *29*

High Court of Australia, *153, 167, 168, 172*

higher education growth, *201*

Higher Education Loan Program (HELP), *200*

higher education providers, see Australian universities,

Higher Education Standards Framework (Threshold Standards) 2015, *66, 67, 69, 71, 73, 88, 90, 92, 94, 100, 101*

Higher Education Support Act 2003 (Cth), *62, 64, 71, 73, 94*

Higher Education Support Amendment 2011, *64, 71*

Holmes, Oliver Wendell, Jr, *118, 121*

Holocaust denial, *176, 188*

Hong Kong, *214*

Honi Soit, *55*

Human Rights Watch (HRW), *214, 216*

Humphreys, Max, *42*

Humphreys Affair 1967 (Sydney University), *41, 42*

Hungarian government, *131*

I

Ian Potter Foundation, *231*

identity politics, *60, 176*

Independent Review of Freedom of Speech in Australian Higher Education Providers, *60, 62, 64, 73, 76, 88, 90, 94, 96, 98, 103, 107, 155, 239, 243* see also Dan Tehan; Robert French; 'Report of the Independent Review of Freedom of Speech in Australian Higher Education Providers',

India, *200, 214*

Indigenous Australians, *55, 183*

Indigenous-rights activism, *56*
  see also 1967 referendum; Charles Perkins (Aboriginal activist); Student Action for Aborigines (SAFA) Freedom Ride 1965,

Indonesia, *201*

Ingwerson, Mr, *2*
  see also Labor clubs; The Age,

Institute of Public Affairs, *6, 239*
  see also 'Free Speech on Campus Audit 2018,
' intellectual freedom, *6, 62, 73, 81, 85, 87, 155*

intellectual inquiry, *111, 118*
  see also free intellectual inquiry,

'intramural expression', *151*

J

Jackson, Robert H. (former US Supreme Court justice), *165*

Jacobs, J. Bruce (Monash emeritus professor), *211*

James Cook University, *148*
  see also Centre of Excellence for

Coral Reef Science; Peter Ridd, James Cook University Enterprise Agreement 2013-2016, *73, 155*

K

Kaiser, Thomas (physicist), *29*
see also Communist Party of Australia; University of New England,
Karmel, Peter (former Flinders University vice-chancellor), *50*
King's College London, *177*
Klein, Tony (physicist), *223*

L

Labor clubs, *2, 4, 9, 11, 12, 47*

see also under Monash University; University of Melbourne; University of Sydney,
Liberal clubs, *33*
see also under University of Melbourne; University of Sydney,
left-wing politics, *6, 17, 22, 58*
lehrfreiheit and lernfreiheit, *136*
liberalism, *163, 170, 172*
Lowe, Charles (former Melbourne University chancellor), *15, 17, 22*

M

MacKinnon, Catherine (feminist scholar), *180, 181*
Makinson, Richard (physicist), *34*

see also Communist Party of Australia; University of Sydney,

Marks, Russell (historian), *46*

May ', *103*

McCarthy era, *58*

McCarthyism, *15*

McKell, William (Australian Labor Party), *9*

McKnight, David (historian), *17, 18*

Medley, John (former Melbourne University vice-chancellor), *22, 24*

Menzies, Robert, *18, 22, 31, 43, 46, 55*
see also Committee on Australian Universities 1957,

Menzies government, *15, 58*

Merck & Co., *222*

Mill, John Stuart, *124, 126, 127, 170, 183, 185, 186*

Model Code, *94, 96, 98, 239, 243, 250, 252, 253, 255*

Monash University, *209, 211*
Council, *42, 43*
ethics policy, *87, 88*
Labor Club, *47*
mass meetings, *38*
student protest 1968, *42, 43*

Murdoch University, *193*
student code of conduct, *193*

Murray, Keith, *22*
see also British University Grants Committee; Committee on Australian Universities 1957,

N

National Health and Medical Research Council, *113, 218, 220*

National Liberation Front of South Vietnam (NLF), 47

national security, 170, 198

National Service Act 1964 (Cth), 46

Nazism, 15

New Education Fellowship, 27

New South Wales parliament, 9

New South Wales Police Special Branch, 31

New York Times Co. v Sullivan, 244

New Zealand, 74, 76
see also Education Act 1989 (NZ),

Newman, John Henry (The Idea of a University), 111

O

Oakeshott, Michael (philosopher), 111, 113

O'Neil, W.M., 27

Oxford University, 113, 151

P

pacifism, 8, 9

Paul Ramsay Foundation, 231
see also The Ramsay Centre,

Perkins, Charles (Aboriginal activist), 55, 56
see also Department of Aboriginal Affairs; Student Action for Aborigines (SAFA) Freedom Ride 1965 University of Sydney,

Peterson, Jordan (psychologist), 103

political left, 6, 17, 22, 58

political liberalism, 163, 170, 172

political rhetoric, 163

political right, 6, 60

Powell, Enoch (Conservative Party politician), *60*

Priestly, Raymond (former Melbourne University vice-chancellor), *11, 12*

'Principles of the Code', *252, 253*

Princeton University, *257*

public debate, *9, 11, 12, 15, 38, 77, 79, 87, 126, 144, 146, 148, 150, 151, 153, 155, 156, 158, 161, 163, 181, 188, 246*
  see also debate,

Public Service Board (Wallace Wurth), *31*

'public square', *96, 98, 167, 168, 185, 186, 188, 190, 192, 244, 253*

Q

Queen's College Oxford, *8*

Queensland, *168*

R

revolution, Paris, *37*

Racial Discrimination Act 1975 (Cth), *168, 170, 176, 253*

racism, *47, 55, 60, 183*

Rangiah, Darryl (Federal Court justice), *155*

religion, *27, 165, 174, 181, 183*

'Report of the Committee on Freedom of Expression',
  see Chicago Principles,

'Report of the Independent Review of Freedom of Speech in Australian Higher Education Providers', *73, 90, 92, 94, 100, 101, 103, 107, 136, 250, 252*
  see also Model Code,

research, *64, 71, 73, 74, 77, 105, 136, 139, 140, 148, 150, 151, 153, 161, 165, 181, 183, 207, 209, 233*
  see also Australian Code for Responsible Conduct of Research 2018 Haldane Principle,
  and academic freedom, *71, 73, 81, 83, 109, 116, 122, 124, 131, 133, 146, 148, 207, 214*
  benefits and value of, *113, 115, 116, 118, 129, 131, 223*
  and ethics, *81, 121, 122, 226, 228, 233, 235*
  funding and challenges, *218, 220, 233, 235, 237*
  funding and partnerships, *196, 198, 200, 222, 223, 226, 228, 237*
  funding and philanthropic donations, *229, 231*
  funding from government, *20, 22, 58, 64, 113, 196, 198, 218, 220*
  funding grants, *113, 216, 218*
  and independence, *124*
  and integrity, *83, 156*
  and methods, *121, 122, 124, 126, 127*
  and the Model Code, *252, 253, 255*
  and policies, *85, 87, 88*
researchers, *22, 83, 115, 118, 121, 122, 124, 136, 140, 198, 209, 218, 220, 222, 226, 228, 235*
Richardson, Sophie (Human Rights Watch), *214*
Ridd, Peter (geophysicist), *73, 148, 150, 155, 156*
  see also Federal Circuit Court; Full Court of the

Federal Court;
James Cook
University,
right-wing politics,
6, 60
RMIT University
academic freedom
statement, *81, 83, 85*
Robertson,
Reverend J. Gray,
11
RSL, *47*

S
Saudi Arabia, *216*
Saunders, Nicholas
(TEQSA chief
commissioner), *71, 73*
School of
International and
Public Affairs, *188*
   see also Columbia
   University,
Searle, John
(University of
California
professor), *41*
Smith, Evan, *58, 60*

social media, *60, 85,
153, 158, 161, 180*
   see also Twitter,
socialism, *9*
Soviet Union, *15*
Spanish Civil War
debate 1937, *9, 11, 12*
   see also Campion
   Society; Charles
   Lowe; Labor
   clubs; Manning
   Clark; Reverend
   J. Gray
   Robertson;
   University of
   Melbourne,
Speak Freely: Why
Universities Must
Defend Freedom of
Speech (Keith
Whittington), *257*
Spry, Charles
(former ASIO
director-general), *18*
St Andrew's
College, University
of Sydney, *9*
'Statement on
Equity, Diversity

and Excellence'
2006, 250
  see also
  University of
  Toronto,
Statement on
Freedom of
Expression,
  see Chicago
  Principles,
'Statement on
Freedom of Speech'
1992, 101, 248
  see also
  University of
  Toronto,
STEMM disciplines,
113
Stone, Geoffrey
(First Amendment
scholar), 241, 243
Storey, John
(former Labor
politician), 9
Student Action for
Aborigines (SAFA)
Freedom Ride 1965,
55, 56

Student Action for
the Rights of
Students (SARS),
41, 42
student protests, 2,
4, 6, 8, 15, 17, 37, 38, 43, 46, 51,
53, 55, 58, 60, 105, 190, 192
  abolition of White
  Australia policy, 55
  American
  civil-rights
  movement, 55, 56
  Columbia
  University
  protests 1967, 37,
  43
  Commonwealth
  Department of
  National Services,
  Sydney, 38
  Department of
  Labour and
  National Service,
  Adelaide, 47
  Martin Place
  Sydney apartheid
  protests, 55

May '68 revolution, Paris, *37*

Monash University mass meetings, *38*

Monash University student protest 1968, *42, 43*

national day of action against conscription and Vietnam War, *50*

Perth student march, *38*

Student Action for Aborigines (SAFA) Freedom Ride 1965, *55, 56*

Students for Democratic Action, Adelaide, *38*

Tlatelolco massacre, Mexico City, *37*

University of California Free Speech Movement 1964, *43*

University of New South Wales students for university management, *38*

University of Queensland student civil-rights march, *37, 38*

University of Sydney Humphreys Affair 1967, *41, 42*

and the Vietnam War, *46, 47, 50, 51, 53, 55*

students, *66, 92, 96, 186, 229, 231, 237, 250, 258*

see also student protests, and academic freedom, *74, 79, 140, 142, 144, 148, 165, 168, 255, 257*

and diversity, *67, 209, 211, 214, 216*

and freedom of speech, *255, 257*

the freedom to learn (lernfreiheit), 135, 136, 139
and harmful speech, 174, 176, 177, 180, 181, 183, 190, 192
the Model Code, 252, 253
and representative bodies, 90, 103
and student fees, 196, 200, 201, 204, 205, 207
university codes and policies, 83, 85, 87, 98, 100, 101, 103, 105, 107, 193, 194
value of university education, 111, 127, 133
Students for Democratic Action, 38
Sydney University of Technology, 29

T
Taiwan, 214
Tasmanian government 1951, 20
teaching, 41, 64, 67, 71, 73, 74, 77, 85, 105, 109, 111, 115, 127, 156, 158, 222, 246, 248, 255
and academic freedom, 131, 133, 135, 139, 146, 148, 150, 165
advancement of knowledge, 140
in the classroom, 135, 136, 142, 144
expectations of students, 204, 205, 207
freedom to learn (lernfreiheit), 131, 133, 135
freedom to teach (lehrfreiheit), 105, 133, 135, 139, 142, 144
and funding partnerships, 229, 231, 233, 237
and the Model Code, 252

and the multicultural classroom, 209, 211, 214
and teaching expertise, 151, 153
Tehan, Dan (education minister), 88
TEQSA (Tertiary Education Quality and Standards Agency), 66, 67, 71, 73
TEQSA Guidance Notes for Higher Education Standards Framework (Threshold Standards) 2015, 67, 69, 71
 'Diversity and Equity', 69
 'Wellbeing and 'Safety', 69, 71
Tertiary Education Quality and Standards Agency Act 2011 (Cth), 66, 71

Tertiary Education Quality and Standards Agency (TEQSA), see under TEQSA (Tertiary Education Quality and Standards Agency),
The Age, 2, 4, 22, 24, 38, 42, 43
The Argus, 15
The Australian, 214
The Brisbane Courier, 25
The Bulletin, 37
'The Fight for World Supremacy' lecture (F.L. Edmunds), 33
The Harm in Hate Speech (Jeremy Waldron), 181
The Idea of a University (John Henry Newman), 111
The Minderoo Foundation, 229
The Ramsay Centre, 231

see also Paul Ramsay Foundation,

The Sun, *43*

The Sydney Morning Herald, *25*

Tlatelolco massacre, Mexico City, *37*

transgender rights, *176*

Twitter, *153, 161*

U

United Kingdom, *8, 98, 100, 177*

  and counterterrorism laws, *170*

  Education Reform Act 1988 (UK), *74, 76*

  Equality and Human Rights Commission, *100, 190*

  Haldane Principle, *218*

United States, *98, 103, 177, 216, 243*

First Amendment law, *244, 246, 248*

First Amendment to the Constitution, *239, 244, 246*

  and Geoffrey Stone (First Amendment scholar), *241*

  and US consulate, Melbourne, *51*

  and US consulate, Sydney, *55*

United States Supreme Court, *165*

Universal Declaration of Human Rights, *87*

Universities Australia, *94*

university governance, *41, 43, 50, 146, 150, 151, 153, 156, 158, 255*

  see also Australian universities,

University of Adelaide, *34, 50*

University of California, *41, 43*
  see also Free Speech Movement 1964,

University of Chicago, *105, 107, 241, 243, 255, 257*
  see also Chicago Principles ('Report of the Committee on Freedom of Expression'); John Ellison (College of University of Chicago),

University of Melbourne, *2, 9, 12, 15, 17, 20, 22, 31, 51, 53, 55, 113*
  see also Charles Lowe; John Medley; Mr Ingwerson; Raymond Maxwell Crawford; Raymond Priestly; Spanish Civil War debate 1937,

Council, *15, 17, 43, 77*

Labor Club, *2, 4, 9, 11, 12*
  see also Mr Ingwerson; The Age,

Liberal Club, *33*
  see also F.L. Edmunds ('The Fight for World Supremacy' lecture),

policy on academic freedom of expression, *81*

policy on student conduct, *87*

policy on workplace behaviour, *153*

Students' Representative Council, *24*

University of Melbourne Act 2009 (Vic.), *77*

University of New England, *29, 31*

University of New South Wales, *29, 34, 38*
  staff code of conduct, *193*
  students for university management, *38*
University of Newcastle, *211, 214*
University of Queensland, *37, 38, 222, 231, 233*
  see also CSL Ltd; Jian Zhou; Gardasil; GlaxoSmithKline PLC.; Merck & Co.; Ian Frazer, student civil-rights march, *37, 38*
University of Southern Queensland code of conduct, *87*
University of Sydney, *8, 27, 31, 34, 51, 55, 113, 214*
  see also Charles Perkins; Richard Makinson; George Wood; Raymond Maxwell Crawford, Freethought Society, *24, 25*
  see also John Anderson, Humphreys Affair 1967, *41, 42*
  see also Max Humphreys; Student Action for the Rights of Students (SARS), Labor clubs, *47*
  Libertarian Society, *24, 25*
  St Andrew's College, *9*
University of Toronto, *248*
University of Western Australia, *85, 153*
  code of conduct, *85, 153*

V

Victoria, *168*

Vietnam War, *46, 47, 50, 51, 53, 55*
  see also
  conscientious
  objectors;
  conscription;
  Department of
  Labour and
  National Service;
  Gorton
  government;
  National Service
  Act 1964,

Voltaire, *165*

W

Waldron, Jeremy
(The Harm in Hate
Speech), *181*

Ward, Russel
Braddock
(Australian
historian), *29, 31*
  see also
  Communist Party
  of Australia; New
  South Wales

Police Special
Branch; Sydney
University of
Technology;
University of New
England,

Western Allies, *15*

White Australia
policy, *55*

Whitlam, Gough, *43, 53, 55*

Whittington, Keith
(Speak Freely: Why
Universities Must
Defend Freedom of
Speech), *257*

Wilfrid Laurier
University, *103*

Wood, George, *8*
  see also
  Australian
  Anti-War League;
  Boer War;
  University of
  Sydney,

World War I, *8*
  see also
  conscription,

World War II, *15*

Wurth, Wallace (Public Service Board), 31

Z

Zhou, Jian (virologist), 222

www.ingramcontent.com/pod-product-compliance
Lightning Source LLC
Chambersburg PA
CBHW011302210326
41599CB00036B/7095